FELTED ANIMAL KNITS

20 keep-forever friends to knit, felt and love

CATHERINE ARNFIELD

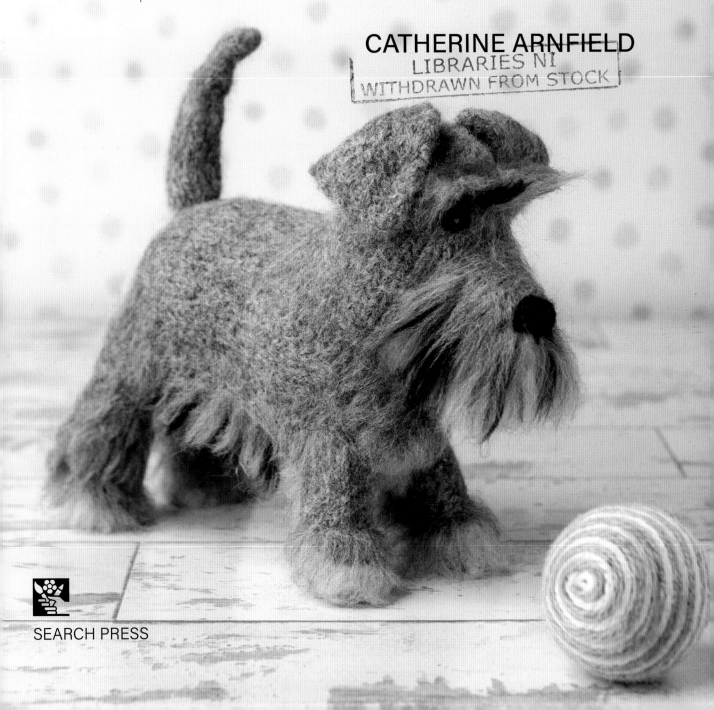

SEARCH PRESS

CONTENTS

Projects

PEANUT & CRUNCH THE MICE 60

PICKLE THE DACHSHUND 66

COCOA & WAFFLE THE ALPACAS 74

SAVANNA THE LION 98

TRUFFLE THE PIG &
JELLYBEAN THE PIGLET 106

TWIGLET THE KOALA 114

ROSEMARY & THYME
THE SQUIRRELS 142

BISCUIT THE SCHNAUZER 148

PAPRIKA THE HIGHLAND COW 154

INTRODUCTION

Since I was a tiny, I have loved all things creative – from drawing and painting to sculpting and model making. I learnt a lot of 'traditional' crafting skills from my parents and grandparents, who knew how to 'make do and mend' and showed me that creating something new was always a possibility.

My love of textiles, in particular, began back in 1993 when I was at college in Chesterfield in Derbyshire, UK. From there I went on to Manchester Metropolitan University to study Textile Design, and this influenced my teaching career in Art and Design greatly before the birth of Knit2Felt – a company I founded in 2017, and still run today – to make designs that fuse knitting with felting.

The idea of combining the arts of knitting and felting came from a desire to knit something that was more realistic in appearance. I had tried knitting, wet felting and needle felting as separate projects, but the light bulb moment came after acquiring some 100 per cent wool yarn then knitting with it and shrinking the design on purpose – much like shrinking your favourite jumper by mistake!

After this moment I was on a roll, and started to create all sorts of animals – knitting and wet felting them as I had before, but then adding their details through needle felting. High Peak in Derbyshire, UK, where I live, is a fantastic place for inspiration as it is surrounded by wildlife, and I soon built up a large collection of designs ready to be put into kits for the launch of Knit2Felt.

One of the advantages of fusing knitting with felting is I found I was able to create bigger projects than I could have done through needle felting alone, by creating the main shapes of the animals through knitting. Another advantage was that it also took away the 'guess work' of building a form from scratch, and eliminated the need for using metal armatures for posing.

This book has gathered together a wide selection of animals, from furry household companions such as cats and dogs to the more exotic, including a lion and a koala. So, there are creatures inside to please everyone's tastes! With every animal I have tried to capture their character, and to ensure this is something you can do too in the easy-to-follow instructions.

It has been an absolute pleasure writing this book, and I hope you enjoy it as much as I have enjoyed making it.

Catherine x

MATERIALS

I love knitting to felt, because all the different gorgeous yarns and fibres you find can be combined! There is now so much available that it's quite easy to source what you need for any project. It is great to experiment, so I have tried to use a wide range of colours and textures to complement the designs in this book.

It is a joy to see a knitted animal transform into something really artistic and more realistic, just using a mixture of yarns and fibres.

YARN

You will need to ensure that the yarn you use is hand-wash only and not treated in any way, as this makes the animals easier to felt. For the same reason, avoid anything which contains man-made fibres such as acrylic and nylon, and keep away from any which is labelled 'super-wash.' The yarns that I have used for these projects are all made with 100 per cent wool, and I have used a selection of DK (light worsted) and aran (worsted) weight yarns from various suppliers. Woolyknit (woolyknit.com), based in Diggle, Lancashire in the UK, has a fantastic range of both yarn and felting fibres (see 'Wool Tops & Roving', right), which you can order easily online.

WOOL TOPS & ROVING

Wool tops are semi-processed fibres – the fleece is cut from sheep and is then washed with the fibres combed in the same direction to produce continuous, smooth, soft lengths of wool. As wool tops are finer, smoother fibres, I like to use them for the needle-felted detailing (see page 38). Fibres from Merino sheep are very soft, and ideal for this purpose. Roving is a fuzzier, textured version of wool tops, whereby the fibres are carded instead of combed. The fibres are also carded in different directions, forcing the fibres to face different directions too, which creates a fluffier texture. Because of this, roving is sometimes referred to as 'carded wool.' The wool from Corriedale sheep tends to fall into this group, as they have a fluffier, slightly coarser texture.

NATURAL FLEECE

Some designs may refer to 'natural fleece.' This is wool in its most 'natural' form – cut from the sheep and washed only. For this reason, fleece appears mainly in cream, brown and grey colours. Cream is the shade I use most often, on the tummy of the schnauzer or to cover the body of the white alpaca. When sourcing fleece, bear in mind that it is referred to as 'core wool' by some needle felting suppliers.

TOY STUFFING/ POLYESTER FIBREFILL

I always use a polyester toy stuffing that meets the current safety standards. It is really easy to use and can be manipulated into the smallest of spaces.

Wool tops

Toy stuffing/
polyester fibrefill

Yarn

Roving

Fleece

EQUIPMENT

There is minimal equipment needed for the projects in this book and there is no need to spend a fortune on an expensive kit to get started. You may already have knitting needles, and felting needles are now becoming a lot easier to buy – they can be found without difficulty online, or in well-stocked craft or haberdashery shops.

KNITTING NEEDLES

Depending on the design you are working on, you will need either 4mm (UK 8; US 6) or 5mm (UK 6; US 8) needles. I prefer to use single-point needles, but do use whatever you are comfortable with.

If a design requires DK (light worsted) weight yarn, then use 4mm (UK 8; US 6) needles; for the aran (worsted) weight projects use 5mm (UK 6; US 8). There is no need to adjust these sizes of needles for tension if you tend to be a tighter or looser knitter, as all knitted pieces will be felted – another advantage!

NEEDLE-FELTING NEEDLES

Felting needles are long, barbed needles with an industrial appearance. When stabbing fibres into place (known as 'needle felting') the barbs, or notches, down the shaft of the pointed end of the needle pull the fibres into the felted knitted piece and catch on the wool. When this action is done repeatedly, it will form felted wool with the fibres. The needles are available in different gauges, from very fine to thicker, robust ones. The finer needles are great for smaller details, and the larger ones are good for working across bigger areas. I use triangular felting needles in only three different gauges – fine (40), medium (38) and coarse (32).

SEWING NEEDLES

A sharp tapestry needle is ideal for sewing up all the different parts of your animals, before and after felting. As you will use yarn to sew up your animals, a large needle with a large eye is easier to use for threading, especially for the aran (worsted) weight yarn.

NEEDLE-FELTING FOAM PAD, OR RICE BAG

There are certain details that will require a surface to needle-felt onto, as the area you are working on will either be thin enough to allow the needle to go all the way through or will be at an awkward angle – from small body parts like ears (see page 54) or the detailing around a tail (see page 55). In these circumstances, in order to protect your needles from blunting or becoming damaged – and from potentially hurting yourself too! – you should felt onto a special needle-felting foam pad or a rice bag. I prefer to use a rice bag – a sock filled with rice will work just as well. Just ensure that your sock is cotton or synthetic and does not contain wool; otherwise, your work will end up attached to the sock!

SCISSORS

A small pair of sharp fabric scissors are handy to keep close by: the designs in this book require yarn to be snipped and felting fibres to be trimmed quite frequently, so these are an essential bit of kit.

STITCH MARKER

To mark areas of knitting, helping you sew up your animals correctly at Stage 2.

METAL WIRE

By inserting wire into particular wet-felted features, such as horns (see page 33), you can bend them into your chosen shapes much more easily. The wire needs to be firmer than floristry wire, so that it will resist as it is threaded through the felt horn. A 1.5mm (0.06in/15 gauge) wire is ideal, and available from hardware stores.

NYLON FISHING WIRE

This is used for whiskers (see page 57).

FINGER PROTECTORS

These are made from leather, and are handy if you are working with a needle-felting needle for a long time. They can be sourced readily online.

PINS

Large dressmaking pins are ideal.

WASHING-UP BOWL, WASHING-UP LIQUID & FLEECE-LINED RUBBER GLOVES

All of these are for wet felting your animals. See pages 29–33 for more information on this.

THE KNIT BIT

I have tried to make sure that the knitting part of the projects in this book is as simple and straightforward as possible. I use a combination of knit (k) and purl (p) stitches, a mix otherwise known as stocking/stockinette stitch, with simple increasing and decreasing to create the shapes.

ABBREVIATIONS

cm	centimetre(s)	kfb	knit into front and back of the same stitch (1 st increase)	st(s)	stitch(es)
cont	continue			St st	stocking/stockinette stitch
dec	decrease(ing)	p	purl		
foll	following, or subsequent	p2tog	purl two stitches together	turn	turn your knitting as instructed, before reaching the end of the row
in	inch(es)	RS	right side		
k	knit	rem	remain(ing)		
k2tog	knit two stitches together (1 st dec)	sl	slip stitch from one needle to another	WS	wrong side

CASTING ON

MAKING A SLIP KNOT

1. Cross the tail end of the yarn over the ball end of the yarn to make a loop.

2. Bring the tail end through the loop.

3. Pull. You've made a slip knot! Pulling the tail end, once the knot is made, will make the loop smaller.

THUMB CAST ON

One of the simplest ways of casting on, and the one my grandmother and mother taught me! Whenever you cast on, ensure that you pull a tail of yarn from your ball that is three times the width of the project you are knitting.

4. Slide the slip knot onto your needle with the ball-end length of the yarn facing towards you. Tighten the slip knot. Wind the tail of yarn around your thumb anticlockwise, as shown.

5. Insert the needle through the loop on your thumb 'knitwise' (from bottom–upwards at the back of your thumb).

6. Wind the ball end length of yarn around the needle anticlockwise.

7. Bring the needle back through the loop, towards the front. This starts to makes a stitch on the needle.

8. Slide your thumb out of the loop and pull the ball end length of yarn to tighten. A new stitch is on the needle.

9. Repeat to cast on the necessary number of stitches required in the pattern.

KNIT STITCH

Knit stitch is the stitch that we are first taught when learning how to knit anything. It forms the 'backbone' of most projects, and is referred to for all the subsequent variations that make new stitches.

Continuous rows of knit stitch are sometimes referred to as garter stitch, which is often used to create knitting with extra texture.

1. With the yarn at the back of the work, insert the right-hand needle through the front of the first stitch on the left-hand needle (this is called 'inserting the needle knitwise').

2. Wind the yarn over the right-hand needle.

3. Bring the wound needle through the loop towards the FRONT – this will start a new stitch on the right-hand needle.

4. Slip the original stitch off the left-hand needle to finish making your new stitch.

- TIP -
When you work one row of knit followed by one row of purl, this is known as stocking/stockinette stitch. This creates a lovely, flat, even texture across the front and back of your work.

PURL STITCH

Purl stitch is very similar to knit stitch, the only difference is that it is made through the 'front' of the stitch.

1. With the yarn at the front of the work, insert the right-hand needle through the front of the first stitch on the left-hand needle (this is called 'inserting the needle purlwise').

2. Wind the yarn over the right-hand needle.

3. Bring the wound needle through the loop towards the BACK – this will start a new stitch on the right-hand needle.

4. Slip the original stitch off the the left-hand needle to finish making your new stitch.

DECREASING

This is known as 'knit two stitches together' (k2tog). Just as it sounds, simply knit two stitches to make them into one stitch on the right-hand needle! See how the needle is sliding through two stitches at once?

- TIP -

You will use k2tog to decrease your work on a knit row. This slants your work to the right. To decrease your work on a purl row, which will slant it to the left, simply work p2tog – you guessed it! It is purling two stitches together.

INCREASING

There are a couple of ways of increasing. Below are two that I use to make the patterns in this book.

The first increase is known as 'knit through front and back of the loop' (kfb), or sometimes 'increase one stitch' (Inc1). This is a subtle, single-stitch increase. You will start to make a knit stitch as per usual, but instead of sliding the stitch off the left-hand needle to finish, you knit into the stitch again – this time through the back of the stitch. You can then slip the stitch off the needle as before.

The second increase, the 'cast-on increase', is even simpler, and requires only casting on extra stitches! This is for sections of knitting that require a dramatic increase in length.

KFB INCREASE

1. With the yarn at the back of the work, insert the right-hand needle through the front of the first stitch on the left-hand needle.

2. Wind the yarn over the right-hand needle and then bring the wound needle through the loop towards the front, as usual.

3. Don't lift the stitch off the needle. Instead, swing the needle up and take it down through the same stitch (the back of the loop). Wind the yarn around the needle.

4. Bring the wound needle through the loop towards the front. You'll see two stitches are now on the needle. Lift the original stitch off the left-hand needle to finish making your two new stitches.

CAST-ON INCREASE

WHAT TO DO: At the beginning of the row, use the working yarn (attached to the knitting) to cast on the number of stitches required in the pattern onto the right-hand/working needle. Once these are on the needle, follow the rest of the pattern instructions to continue working the rest of the knitting.

CASTING/BINDING OFF – 'FLAT' KNITTING

Casting/binding off secures your knitted piece after you have finished knitting it, stopping it from unravelling. In addition, it leaves you with a 'tail' of yarn which you can use to sew the piece to another knitted section later.

There are two ways I like to cast/bind off my animals, depending on the shape of the piece I am knitting. On this page, I will show you how to cast/bind off a 'flat' piece of knitting. The example here shows casting/binding off knitwise; purlwise casting/binding off is exactly the same, except the two stitches on the needle are purled!

1. Knit the first two stitches in the usual way (see page 14).

2. Using the tip of the left needle, insert it into the front of the first stitch knitted, so that the tip is pointing from the bottom left to the top right corner.

3. Pass this stitch your left-hand needle has picked up over the second stitch knitted.

4. Drop the secured stitch off the needle.

5. Work the next stitch so that there are two stitches on the right-hand needle again. Repeat steps 2–5 to the end of the row until only one stitch remains on the right-hand needle.

6. Cut the yarn, leaving a 10cm (4in) length. Carefully slip the last stitch off the needle, then pull the cut length through the loop and tighten.

Finished cast-/bound-off work.

CASTING/BINDING OFF
– 'GATHERED' KNITTING

(BREAKING AND THREADING THROUGH YARN)

I use this technique a lot in my designs to cast/bind off 'rounded' or shaped pieces of knitting, such as a head or foot. I like to use a large, pointed tapestry needle to complete this task.

1. With your work still on the needle, take the working end of your yarn and cut it, leaving a long tail. Thread the tail through your tapestry needle. Push the needle through all the stitches on your top, final row.

2. Once the needle is pushed all the way through, all the stitches should be temporarily secure on the tail of yarn. Pull the threaded needle upwards and carefully slide the piece of knitting off the knitting needle.

3. Continue to pull the yarn tightly, towards your right hand. See how the top of the piece has started to shape into a point, now that the stitches are gathered together?

Finished cast-/bound-off work.

4. At the 'beginning' end of the top row of knitting, start to secure the shape by sewing through one or two stitches with a tapestry needle.

5. Pull the needle once more to draw the top row together.

DIAGRAMS

To help you piece together and sew up your animals at Stage 2 (see overleaf), I have created diagrams to accompany each creature. There is one diagram for each animal with its separate, knitted components, and another of the finished, assembled animal. Annotations will appear beside the individual body parts, too. Each creature is sewn up in a slightly different way, depending on the shape of their body. The examples below show the two most common shapes.

KEY

1. *Leave a gap for stuffing.*

2. *Edges of knitting are brought together and sewn in place with whipped/overcast stitching.*

3. *Body part with no markings – cast/bound off as usual, then the yarn tails are simply sewn in. No further sewing up required.*

4. *Arrows show that these sections of the body need to be brought together then sewn in place to hold and secure the shape. (For more details, see page 23.)*

5. *Once the two sections are sewn together, some animals will need to have a 'dart' sewn across their bottoms afterwards, to round the shape. (For more details, see page 23.)*

Body made of several pieces.

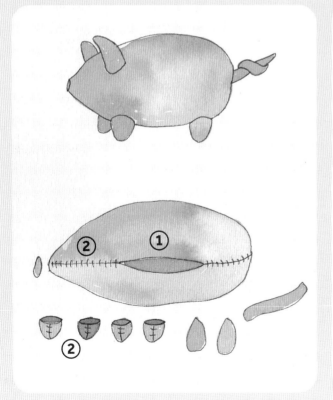

Body made mostly all in one.

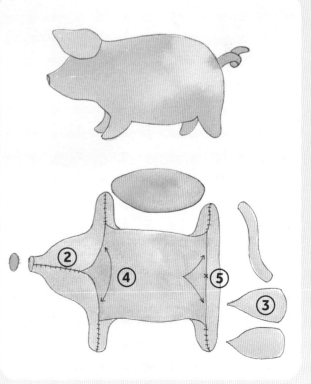

19

SEWING UP

Sewing up the pieces before felting is essential. This makes sure that you will achieve the desired shape and size of your animal, so that it is ready for assembly and detailing later.

Because all the knitted pieces will be felted you do not have to be the neatest of sewer-uppers! The pieces will shrink, the knitted stitches will blend together and, especially if your creature is felted enough, almost all your stitching will 'disappear'.

To sew up your animals, simply use the tails of yarn remaining from casting/ binding off. There is no particular stitch that I recommend to sew up your animals – as long as they are secure and made closely together, they'll be perfect for felting later! I like to use whip/overcast stitch – sewing back and forth along the edges to be joined – this is the method I will be using throughout this chapter.

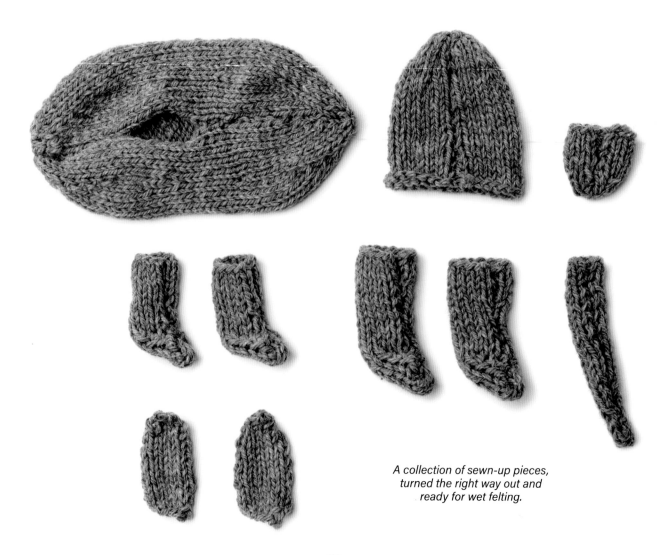

A collection of sewn-up pieces, turned the right way out and ready for wet felting.

BODIES

The bodies of the animals in this book are made using one of two methods. The first method is to knit the body separately from the legs (which are then sewn onto the body later) so the only sewing up needed is the gap around its tummy. The second method is where the head and legs are knitted in the same piece as body – the head and legs then need to be 'shaped' and sewn up at the same time as the body.

FIRST METHOD – SEPARATE BODY PIECE

1. Hold the row ends together with the right sides facing (so the body is inside out). Mark out a section to leave unstitched with either your hands or pins, for stuffing into later. Depending on the size of the animal, this will range from 2–6cm (¾–2½in) in length.

2. Thread the cast/bind off tail onto a tapestry needle and take it through the top row of edge stitches, across the gap, to bring them together.

3. Pull firmly to secure the first stitch.

4. Now take the needle below this first stitch, from the opposite to the starting side. Pull firmly to secure the second stitch. Repeat this process down to the marked opening, on both ends of the body. Once finished, follow the instructions on page 28 to sew in and cut off the loose ends.

Finished sewn-up body. Simply turn it right side out, through the stuffing gap, and then it's ready for wet felting.

SECOND METHOD –
ALL-IN-ONE BODY PIECE

With this method, I advise following the diagram of the animal carefully. If necessary, gently pin the sections together first to ensure you have joined them correctly. As with the separate body piece on the previous page, ensure that you leave a small opening along the tummy for stuffing into later.

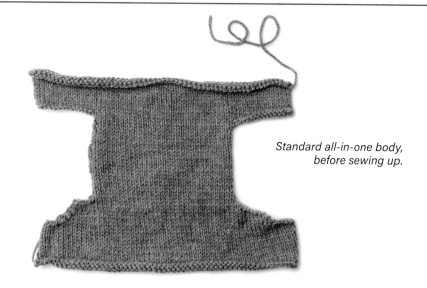

Standard all-in-one body, before sewing up.

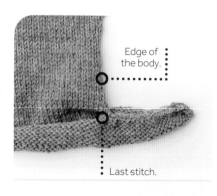

Edge of the body.

Last stitch.

1. At one leg, hold the row ends together (this makes the shape of the foot) with the right sides facing. Thread a 30cm (12in) length of yarn from the ball used to knit the animal onto a tapestry needle and take it through the stitches at the ends of the rows, across the gap, to bring them together.

2. Pull firmly to secure the first stitch. Now take the needle below this first stitch, from the opposite to the starting side. Pull firmly to secure the second stitch.

3. Repeat the process down the rest of the 'foot'. Bring the leg edges right sides together and sew up the whole edge in the same way described in steps 1 and 2. The final stitch should be aligned with the edge of the body. Once you have finished sewing up the leg, follow the instructions on page 28 to sew in and cut the loose tails of yarn.

Once you have finished sewing up the leg, follow the instructions on page 28 to sew in and cut the loose tails of yarn.

> **- TIP -**
> *For two of the legs, you will be able to use the yarn tails from casting on and casting/binding off earlier to sew them up.*

4. Repeat steps 1–3 for the three remaining legs.

5. Using the diagram to help you, pinch together either the front or hind legs of the animal evenly, right sides together – on the diagram, these will be indicated by the arrows. A pin or two will help hold these sections together before you start to sew!

6. Using the same stitching process described in steps 1 and 2, sew up the section between the two legs, up to the arrow intersection seen on the diagram.

7. Repeat at the other end of the body, with the remaining legs. See how your animal is starting to take shape?

8. For most of the animals with an all-in-one body, you will need to give them a rounder shape, either at the head or tail end, or both. This will be indicated by an 'X' (see page 19). To do this, you will need to make a 'dart'. This is simply sewing a running stitch across the section, from one end to the other along the 'X' marker, while the body is still inside out. For demonstration purposes, I have used a contrasting-coloured yarn, but for your own animal make sure the yarn you sew with is the one you used for knitting.

Finished sewn-up body. Simply turn it right side out, through the stuffing gap, and then it's ready for wet felting.

HEADS

Sometimes the head is in the same piece as the body, such as Truffle the Pig (see page 106), but a number of patterns will ask you to sew a separate head piece onto the body. You should be able to use the yarn tail from casting on to sew up the head.

WHAT TO DO: Sew the row ends of the head together with right sides facing, leaving either the cast-on edge open in a cup shape as shown, or (in the case of Pebble the Seal, see page 90) an opening left midway for stuffing and assembly. Once finished, take the needle down through the worked stitches twice then cut the yarn flush against the knitting. Turn the head piece right side out to finish, so that it is ready for wet felting.

TAILS

These come in all shapes and sizes, and are knitted and sewn up in slightly different ways. However, a typical tail is usually tubular in shape with a pointed end, and you can apply the principles in the steps below to most of the animals in this book. If the tail is slightly different, the instructions in the sewing up stage will explain what to do. Always refer to your diagram for help, too.

I will also show you below how to make a curve in a tubular tail – excellent for a dog with a waggy tail!

Finished curled tail.

1. Bring the long slanted edges of the knitted tail shape right sides together. Sew these slanted edges together, leaving the short bottom edge open, using whip/overcast stitch.

2. Thread up a tapestry needle with a matching-coloured length of yarn that's twice the size of the tail (I have deliberately used a contrasting yarn colour here, for clarity). Bring the needle up at the point of the tail, then wiggle it through the whip/overcast edge of stitching about halfway along the tail.

3. Pull on the threaded yarn. You'll start to see the tail curl up! Once you are happy with your curled tail, anchor the shape in place with a few small whip/overcast stitches. To finish, turn the tail right side out, so that it is ready for wet felting.

LIMBS

Just like the bodies, there are a few ways of making the limbs for your animals. Below are the main types of limbs, but remember each animal's limbs will be made slightly differently. Don't panic! These will explained in detail on the project pages.

'ARMS' OR 'SIMPLE FRONT LEGS'

Typically these are sewn up in the same way as the head – the row ends are brought together and sewn up with whip/overcast stitch, and the cast-on edge is left open for stuffing later. In fact smaller front legs (like those on Paprika the Highland Cow, see below right and on page 154) are essentially small 'heads'.

Occasionally, arms or simple front legs are slanted at the opened end so that, when they are sewn on after wet felting, they fit the contours of the body. These arms or simple front legs tend to be longer, and can be seen on animals like Thyme the Squirrel shown right (see page 142), and Savanna the Lion (see page 98).

Longer, slanted arms/simple front legs on the diagram of Thyme the Squirrel (below) and the final arms on the finished creature (right).

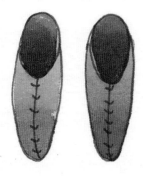

Shorter, regular arms/simple front legs on the diagram of Paprika the Highland Cow (below) and the final front legs on the finished creature (right).

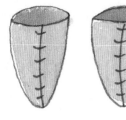

'FOOTED LEGS'

These limbs are made and sewn up like little boots. Depending on the animal, they can be used for all of the legs of a standing animal, or the front legs only. Just like the limbs on page 25, the opening can be slanted to fit the shape of the animal's body.

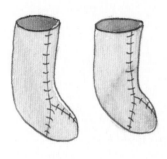

Straight legs on the diagram of Biscuit the Schnauzer.

1. Most of the footed legs start off as a triangular-shaped piece of knitting.

2. Thread up a tapestry needle with a matching-coloured length of yarn that's twice the length of the leg. Bring the long, slanted edges of the triangular shape right sides together. Sew these slanted edges together, leaving the pointed end and cast-on end open, using whip/overcast stitch.

3. Thread the tapestry needle with the cast-/bound-off tail of yarn. Take the needle across the sewn edge, about a quarter of the way up from the point of the leg.

4. Pull on the threaded end of the tail. See how it draws the point in towards the leg? Once it is flush against the leg, work a few whip/overcast stitches at the point to secure. Finish by sewing in and cutting the loose ends (see page 28).

Turn inside out to finish your footed leg.

'SITTING LEGS'

For sitting or lounging animals, such as Twiglet the Koala (see page 114) and Savanna the Lion (see page 98), the leg and foot are knitted in one – like the footed legs – with the lower part of the leg at a 45-degree angle to help your animal sit comfortably on a flat surface. The finished leg leaves you with cup-like foot at the end of the lower limb, for stuffing the foot later.

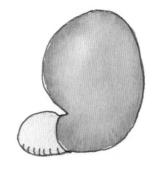

Sitting legs on the diagram of the koala (above left) and the final legs on the finished creature (above right).

Right side of the sitting leg.

Wrong side of the sitting leg.

1. Once you have finished knitting your sitting legs, they should look like the pieces above. The small foot end will be your cast-/bound-off edge, and will leave you with a tail of yarn for sewing the foot partly to the leg.

2. Turn the foot end so it is facing the leg right sides together.

3. Thread the tapestry needle with the cast-/bound-off tail of yarn. Take the needle across the two edges and use whip/overcast stitch as before to bring the edges together at the tip of the foot.

4. Repeat all the way down the foot, until it looks like the image above. Once finished, follow the instructions on page 28 to sew in and cut the loose ends.

Simply turn the foot right way out to complete your sitting leg.

EARS, WINGS & BELLIES

Ears, wings and tummy pieces (these cover the stuffing gap for the all-in-one bodies) are simple '2D' shapes that, once knitted, you simply sew in the cast-on and cast-/bound-off tails. The ear is used as the example in the 'Sewing in loose ends' technique below.

All these body parts can vary in shape, and the detailing that will define your specific animal is done at a later stage, during the needle-felting process.

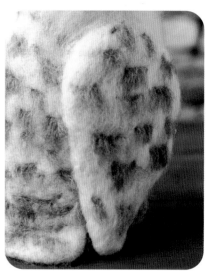

SEWING IN LOOSE ENDS

Any loose ends need to be secured so that they don't get in the way during the wet felting process.

1. Thread the tapestry needle with the tail of yarn either leftover from casting/binding off or from sewing up your edges. Take the needle down through several knitted edge stitches, as shown here, or through the seam you have just finished stitching.

2. Pull the yarn tail firmly to secure, taking care not to distort the shape of your animal. Repeat steps 1 and 2 once more.

3. Once the sewn-up end is secure, cut the yarn flush against the piece of knitting. The yarn should shrink into the stitches, hiding it from sight.

WET FELTING

By wet felting the different knitted parts of your animal, you can produce fantastic effects: the needle-felted 'look' is created more easily; you can give more shape and form to your chosen animal, and the texture made as a result gives a lovely touch of realism to your creature.

Wet felting is a very simple process that is done by hand, requiring only your basic washing-up kit: hot water, rubber gloves and washing-up liquid.

Always work with one piece of knitting at a time.

BASIC FELTING MOTION

LARGE BODY PARTS

1. Fill the bowl with enough water to submerge your knitted pieces, along with a squirt of washing-up liquid. Have the water as hot as you can stand. Fully submerge the knitted piece.

2. 'Swish' the knitting around in the hot soapy water for a few minutes.

3. Lift the knitting out of the water and begin to rub the piece between your hands in all directions. At first the knitting will expand and become very floppy; this is normal, and the knitting will become stiffer and smaller as you repeat the process. Repeat steps 2 and 3 until the knitted stitches are 'invisible' and felted together. Rinse the piece with clean water (this can be cold) then squeeze out the excess water.

Before wet felting and after wet felting (above). The felting process not only forces the fibres to mesh together – so any messy knit or sewing stitches will 'disappear' – but shrinks the knitted piece slightly too.

SMALL BODY PARTS

Smaller pieces of knitting are easier to felt and shape without gloves, but it will mean you'll need slightly cooler water!

1. Submerge and 'swish' the knitting in soapy water that is as hot as you can stand.

2. Depending on the body part, rub or roll the piece between your palms; a lather will start to build. Repeat steps 1 and 2, opposite, until the knitted stitches are 'invisible' and felted together. Rinse the piece with clean water (this can be cold) then squeeze out the excess water.

- TIP -
Lined rubber gloves enable you to work with hotter water. The hotter the water, the quicker the felting process will be.

- TIP -
The more times the swishing and rubbing process is repeated, the more felted the piece will become.

MOULDING & SCULPTING

Once you have squeezed the water out of your knitting, most of your animal's body parts will need moulding while damp to ensure that they dry in the correct shape for stuffing and sewing later.

At this stage, when it is damp, the knitting is very mouldable and can be manipulated into shape very well. Take your time to make sure that you are happy with the form of your body part before leaving it to dry.

When you are happy with the shape of your knitting, leave it to dry naturally if possible – although if your house is on the chilly side, on a towel near a (non-flame) heat source is fine.

FOR HOLLOW PIECES (BODIES, HEADS, LEGS)

Cup it in your hand, stuff with kitchen paper firmly and 'mould' into the desired shape.

FOR FLAT PIECES (EARS, FINS, WINGS)

Flat pieces can be pulled into your desired shape and then dried flat on a clean towel.

EXTRA WET-FELTED FEATURES

Some of the animals in this book will require extra features that will need wet felting before stuffing and construction. These are made with merino wool tops or roving fibres – and so are more like traditional wet felting – but the small amounts you need and the size of the feature make the process an economical and relaxing one.

CURLY LOCKS

These are perfect for the fur of Paprika the Highland Cow (see page 154) – and they could be a fun alternative to use for Cocoa and Waffle the Alpacas (see page 74)! I use mostly merino wool tops to make the fur. You will also need lots of spare knitting needles!

1. Pull off a long, thin section of the merino wool tops, approximately 30cm (12in) long.

2. Dip the length into the hot soapy water.

3. Immediately wrap the wet length tightly around a spare knitting needle. Leave it to dry naturally on a towel, or on a non-flame heat source. Repeat this process to create fifteen to twenty curly locks.

4. Once the length is dry and ready for use, simply slide it off the needle.

> **- TIP -**
>
> *You may need make these in several sessions, depending on how many spare pairs of knitting needles you have!*
>
> *I like to leave them on the needles, even when they've been dry for a long time. This keeps the curl intact, so it is in perfect condition whenever I need it!*

HORNS

Some animals (like Paprika the Highland Cow on page 154) will need horns. These are made from strips of fibres. I tend to use wool roving for my horns, as it has more texture and natural colour variation. You only need to work with one length, as this can be cut into two later if necessary.

1. Cut off an 8cm (3in) length grey wool roving, approximately 4cm (1½in) wide.

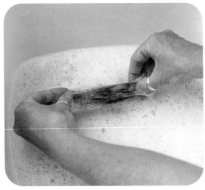

2. 'Swish' the length in a little hot, soapy water.

3. Roll the wet fibres between the palms of your hands, back and forth, until the fibres are fully felted together. Pay attention to the ends to ensure they become pointy. Leave to dry.

4. Once the horns are dry, cut them in half.

5. Cut a 12cm (4¾in) length from a 1.5mm (0.06in/15 gauge) reel of wire and push each end into the flat sections of the horns, pushing them right up to the pointed tips of the felted horns. Do this gently and carefully, to ensure you don't force the wire out through each end!

6. Bend the horns as desired then position over the top of the head. Using matching yarn (here I have used a grey yarn for demonstration purposes), stitch over the wire to secure it in place. I recommend attaching the horns before adding the base fur or extra fur details; you can use these details to cover the wire at the centre later.

STUFFING & CONSTRUCTION

Careful stuffing and assembly is key to creating your amazing
alpaca or lovely lion. I have included assembly diagrams
for all the projects in this book to help with the stuffing and
construction of your projects, providing you with references for
shape and positioning.

STUFFING

It is important that the animals are stuffed firmly. This is to ensure that the
shape does not distort when the needle-felted detailing is added later. It
will also make your animal stiff and stable, and the legs strong and rigid
enough to stand up.

FOR LARGE BODY PIECES (BODIES, HEADS)

Firmly stuff through the opening left
after sewing up (see pages 21–24).

FOR SMALL BODY PIECES (TAILS, LEGS, FEET)

Use the knob end of a knitting
needle to push the stuffing into the
opening. Additional stuffing can be
added at the point of construction
later, before your seams are fully
joined. This is especially effective at
the point of joining limbs.

SEWING UP THE BODY STUFFING GAP

Follow the instructions below to sew up the gap you
left behind for stuffing. Small, close stitches will be more
discreet and even.

1. Thread a 30cm (12in) length of matching
yarn onto a sharp tapestry needle and
knot the end. Take the needle up through
the stuffed piece at the top-left end of the
opening, so that the knot is hidden inside.

2. Take the needle to the right side of the
opening, parallel to the knotted end, and then
bring it down through the piece.

3. Pull the yarn firmly. This will draw the gap
between the two lengths together, and make
the first stitch.

4. Continue to take the needle from left to
right all the way down the opening, firmly
pulling the yarn each time to draw the two
edges together.

5. To finish, work one more stitch in the same
place as the last stitch, then bring the needle
down and out through the whole piece on the
other side.

6. Pull the yarn firmly then cut it flush against
the surface of the piece. The yarn should
shrink back inside the piece.

PINNING

It is really helpful to pin all your pieces into position prior to sewing: it allows you to position the legs and angle bodies correctly, and make sure that your piece will stand up. If you're not happy with the way your animal sits, simply reposition your pieces until the desired pose is achieved.

SEWING

Use small whip/overcast stitches to sew all the pieces together using the same yarn as the knitted piece. The smaller the stitches, the neater your piece will be. Don't worry too much about any visible stitches, as they will likely be covered with the needle felting later.

REGULAR JOINS

1. Thread a 30cm (12in) length of matching yarn onto a sharp tapestry needle and knot the end. Take the needle down through an area close to the join you will be sewing up, then bring the needle out at the area you will be sewing.

2. Pull the yarn until the end just disappears inside the body. Don't pull too hard else the yarn will come straight out again!

3. To the side, work a tiny whip/overcast stitch across the join between the two body pieces.

4. Just above the anchor stitch, work the second whip/overcast stitch as shown.

5. To anchor the stitch in place work another small stitch just below, at a horizontal angle.

6. Repeat the whip/overcast stitching and anchor stitching process all around the join, to secure the two pieces together.

7. To finish, take the needle down through the second body piece and out through the other side. Pull the yarn, then cut flush. The yarn should shrink back inside.

STUFFING JOINS

Some body parts, such as the legs, will require you to stuff the piece partway through sewing, to ensure the join is as full and firm as possible before it is fully attached. Simply sew about three-quarters of the way around, so that there is about a finger-sized stuffing gap left. Then, stuff the remaining space firmly and continue to sew and close up as above.

NEEDLE FELTING & DETAILS

By combining the arts of knitting and felting, unique and realistic effects can be achieved: you can add long fur, realistic eyes, variegated colour and precise detailing that is not achievable with knitting alone – and all with just a needle and some lengths of fibres.

Needle felting also gives you the opportunity to personalize your animal, especially if you have a special creature or pet in mind – simply change the fur type and colour, along with any markings and eye colour, to make an animal that's personal to you.

The equipment you need is quite minimal. A foam pad or a rice bag will be needed for small details to protect your fingers, although a sock with rice in would make a sufficient, economical alternative. Holders are also available for your felting needles, for you to place at the holding end of the needle. These make them more comfortable to use, but are not essential. Finally, have to hand a selection of merino wool tops or roving fibres that match or co-ordinate with your design.

HOW TO HOLD THE NEEDLE

Felting needles are extremely sharp and break the skin very easily, so due care and attention is required. When I am teaching a needle felting class I always state the obvious, which is to never take your eye off the work. It's easy to get distracted and look away from your work, but this is when you are most likely to slip with the needle. Keep your fingers away from the felting area where possible, and hold the needle at the non-pointy end!

Needle holder.

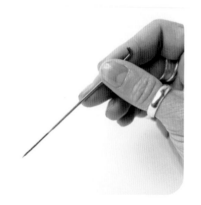

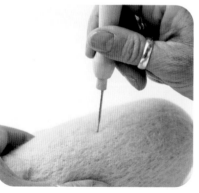

NEEDLE-FELTING MOTION

The needle should be going in at a 90-degree angle to the work with no twisting or bending – this will minimize the chances of the needle breaking. Use a confident 'stabbing' motion to attach the fibres in place – not too hard as, again, this could break the needle.

BASE FUR

LAYING ON FLAT FUR

With the occasional exceptions, most of the projects in this book have a layer of flat fur needle felted all over the body, legs and head. This not only adds to the realism of the animal, it gives him or her more shape and smooths out the whole project, covering up any seaming from sewing up earlier. For animals that aren't particularly hairy (like Truffle the Pig on page 106), or not hairy at all (such as Pebble the Seal on page 90), you still add fibres to the body but give them a much thinner layer than you would for hairier animals, or cover only the obvious seams. Always choose fibre colours that are close to the knitting yarn colour.

> **- TIP -**
>
> *For small areas – such as the legs, ears and tails – use smaller amounts of fibres and work with the foam block or rice bag/sock to protect your fingers.*

> **- TIP -**
>
> *An 8 x 4cm (3 x 1½in) amount of fibres is the largest piece I recommend working with at a time. If it's too big, the fibres can look uneven or look unnatural when needle felted onto the body.*

1. It's best to 'pull' the fibres rather than cutting them, as this leaves you with a nice graduated edge that will blend nicely into the felted knitting, as opposed to a blunt edge that will take more time and effort to blend in. Pull off a small, narrow section of the roving or wool tops, approximately 8cm (3in) long and 4cm (1½in) wide.

2. Open out the fibres into a wide, flat shape to thin it out. Lay them against the area you are working on – here, I'm placing it over the back seam of the animal.

3. To attach the fibres, simply 'stab' them repeatedly in place through the felted knitting, at the point you wish to attach them. Initially secure the fibres with spaced-out stabbing around the edges.

4. Once the fibres are partially secure, the rest of the length can be worked until the fibres lie flat. If there are extra fibres you don't want to needle felt, simply trim into them (a bit like a hair stylist!) with your scissors to shorten them.

LAYING ON 'BOUNCY' FUR

As an alternative to the smooth fur on the previous page, an overall fleecy coat can be needle felted onto your animal. This looks a bit like sheep fleece when finished, and is perfect for animals like Cocoa and Waffle the Alpacas (see page 74).

1. Pull off an 8cm (3in) long and 4cm (1½in) wide piece of roving or fleece and roll it into a ball. This will allow the fibres to remain bouncy and proud after needle felting into place.

2. Lay the ball over the intended area.

- TIP -
Depending on the area, the size of the ball you roll will vary – for example, with heads, needle felt lots of smaller little balls over the knitting to ensure an even and controlled distribution of fur.

3. Start to needle felt the ball of fibres – work the outer area of the ball first to secure it, then work towards the middle.

4. The near-finished needle-felted fur. Note how bouncy and textured it looks?

FUR TEXTURES

Sometimes, your animal's fur will need a little more texture added to it for further realism. Below are the techniques I use most often for most of my animals.

FLUFFY FUR

This is perfect for animals like mice and slightly fluffy pets such as dogs and kittens. This is a technique usually applied to animals with base flat fur (see page 39).

1. With the needle-felting needle, lightly touch the tip on the fur and gently flick it upwards, against the direction of the fur – this is similar to a gentle 'scratching' motion.

2. Repeat here and there across the whole of the body. See how the fur now has a lightly tufty appearance?

CURLY FUR

Add some curls to your creature, using the curly locks made earlier during the wet felting process (see page 32).

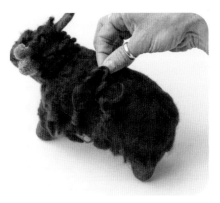

1. Take the dried curly lock and gently pull it apart slightly – this makes the lock look more realistic, and easier to felt.

2. Fold the lock in half. Pinching the fold, lay it over your desired area.

3. Needle felt the folded section to secure the lock initially, then needle felt here and there to secure the rest of the lock in place. Take care not to overdo this – you want the lock to hang loosely a little. Repeat to cover the whole area.

SHORT, TUFTY FUR

Some animals will have short, tufty sections of fur – whether it's along their tummy like Marmalade the Cat (see page 120) or even in their ears like Twiglet the Koala (see page 114)!

1. Pull off an 8cm (3in) length of your chosen fibres, approximately 4cm (1½in) wide. Here, we're adding longer fur along the tummy of the cat.

2. Spread out the fibres to your chosen width, and to thin them out slightly.

3. Approximately 1cm (⅜in) down from the top, needle felt the fibres in place.

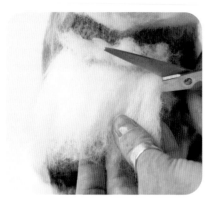

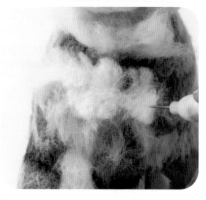

4. Once attached, trim the fur to your chosen length. For Marmalade the Cat, the fur on the tummy doesn't need to be too long, so I am snipping the fibres about 1cm (⅜in) down from the needle-felting line.

5. Fluff up the fibres above and below the needle-felted line with the needle-felting needle.

> **- TIP -**
> The Colour Blending technique on pages 46 and 47 is very similar to this process – you just use more colours!

LONG FUR

Animals like Biscuit the Schnauzer (see page 148) and Savanna the Lion (see page 98) will have longer sections of hair. Long fur is made and added in a very similar way to the short, tufty fur opposite, with only a few adjustments. Depending on the animal, you can leave the ends of the fibre as they are for a natural, graduated look, or trim them straight across in a blunt cut to give your creature a groomed style!

1. Pull off and spread out the same amount of fibre as in steps 1 and 2 opposite, then lay them over your chosen area – here, we are a adding the bottom section of the lion's mane.

2. Needle felt the fur in place, approximately a third of the way down from the top.

3. Fold the top section down over the lower section, then needle felt here and there along the fold line to secure the top layer in place.

4. Repeat the process as many times as needed – as I am making a whole mane for the lion here, I need to add several layers of fibres above the first to cover the whole head.

Finished long fur. See how working from bottom to top allows a gradual, realistic layering of fur?

EXTRA COLOURS, TONES & PATTERNS

A number of animals will need colours mixed into their fur. Sometimes this can be done by adding simple stripes and markings to the base fur; other times, if you are adding short or long fur to your animal, colours will need to blended from one shade to another – this is achieved by mixing lots of thin lengths of different-coloured fibres together.

Always work a small section at time, so that the colours blend both subtly and effectively.

ADDING STRIPES OR MARKINGS

Stripes and markings can be great for adding those individual and special touches to your project. You can use these techniques to personalize your projects, maybe you have your own cat or dog that you wish to recreate in wool?

Gallery of stripes & markings

1. *Raccoon stripes (see also Furry Tail on page 55).*

2. *Owl wing marks, using the Short, Tufty Fur technique on page 42 but on a much smaller scale!*

3. *Cat forehead markings, using the stripes technique.*

4. *Piglet spots, made with brown wool tops, shaped, laid flat and needled into position.*

5. *Owl spots, using natural fleece 'pulled' into small, irregular shapes.*

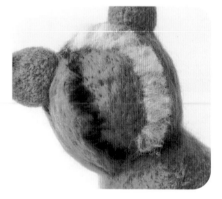

1. Trim a thin length of fibres, cut widthways, from a pull of fibre in your chosen colour.

2. Lay it over the area to be patterned – I am placing this over the head of my cat – then needle felt it into place as usual.

3. Repeat here and there across the body, and using a variety of co-ordinating pieces of fibres. Subtle markings can be added by simply using thinner amounts of fibres and spreading them out slightly before needle-felting.

- TIP -
Cutting across the width of the fibres makes the stripes and patterns blend more subtly when needle felting.

- TIP -
Stripes and markings not only add interest to your animals, but are handy for hiding any seams where the animal has been joined together – especially if the base fur is very thin.

COLOUR BLENDING

Different-coloured lengths of fibres can be laid on top of each other to create new colours or subtle graduations of colour, giving your animal more realism. This technique can be used for any length of fur. For colour blending I tend to use about three different colours, but you can choose your own combination.

- TIP -

If you're new to needle felting and a bit nervous about colour blending, some suppliers of felting wool provide ready-blended mixes of colours – these can be experimented with if you wish!

1. Pull off a small length of your lightest colour.

2. Pull off a thinner amount of your darkest colour and lay this over the top.

3. As with the long fur application (see page 43), needle felt across the fibres to secure them in place, about a third of the way down from the top.

4. Fold the top section down over the lower section.

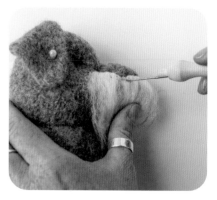

5. Needle felt here and there along the fold line to secure the top layer in place.

6. Thin out the needle-felted layers with the needle by dragging the needle downwards through the fibres. This gets rid of excess volume if the layers look too bulky, and reveals more of the mixed colours, too.

7. If your animal needs a groomed look, trim the ends of the fur.

8. Pull off a small length of fibre that matches the colour of your animal. Fold over the top edge by 1cm (⅜in) or so, then lay this a little way up from the needle-felted fibres.

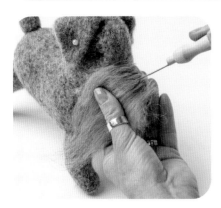

9. Needle felt the top layer in place, along the folded edge.

10. Trim the top layer of fibres to the length of the mix of fibres underneath to finish, holding the scissors at an angle to add a natural texture to fur.

Finished animal (see also page 148). Continue to add more colours over the top in the same way, if you wish, to add further interest.

SCULPTING

Many of your animals will need sculpting to add realistic contouring and shaping. This is usually done once the base fur (if needed) is needle felted in place. Some sculpting can be achieved by manipulating the shape, adding stitches (some visible, some not) such as here, where the eye sockets are being created, or by building up shapes with more felting wool, to make parts such as the cheeks of Marmalade the Cat (see page 120).

EYE SOCKETS

By creating eye sockets you can transform the shape of your animal's face. It is an easy process, and has the added bonus of establishing symmetrical markers for your needle-felted eyes later.

1. Work out where you would like the eyes to be, then mark the areas with pins.

2. Thread a 30cm (12in) length of matching yarn onto a sharp tapestry needle and make a small knot at the end. Make a tiny anchor stitch at the corner of the eye area.

3. Close to the pin, take the needle through the head, close to the pin on the opposite side of the head.

4. Pull tight to make the first indentation.

5. Return to the other side. See how the sockets are starting to form?

6. Repeat the process in the same spots – twice one way, twice on the other. To finish, make one tiny anchor stitch at the centre of the eye then take the needle through to the back of head. Cut the yarn flush.

CHEEKS/MOUTHS

In animals like Marmalade the Cat (see page 120) and Savanna the Lion (see page 98), the 'mouth' area has further fibres added on top to create cheek shapes and mouth indents.

1. Take an 8–10cm (3–4in) length of fibres that match the area to be needle felted. Fold the length in half and shape it until it resembles a flat oval.

2. Pin the shape to one side of the mouth.

3. Needle felt around the edges first to establish the shape. Work with the contours of the head beneath, trying to flatten the outer edges a little to create a nice graduation from body to fibre.

4. Finished cheek section.

5. Repeat steps 1–4 to add the other cheek.

6. To cover and blend the gap between the two cheeks, take a small, thin piece of the same fibres.

7. Lay it horizontally over the whole mouth area, then start to needle felt down the centre, between the two cheeks.

8. Once the central section is secure, needle felt the edges of the thin fibres to finish. To make the mouth, remember to needle a 'V' shape into the bottom!

NOSE

With all the animals, a little extra detailing will be required to create the perfect nose, whether that is simply adding some nostrils or adding more details, such as those on Savanna the Lion (see page 98). All of these details are achieved with needle-felting techniques to add extra shape and dimension. This technique begins that process.

1. Pull a thin, 8–10cm (3–4in) length of fibres that match the body of the animal. Fold over one end by approximately 1cm (⅜in) or so.

2. With the folded side at the bottom and facing down, lay the piece centrally over the nose-to-forehead area.

3. Starting from the 'top' of one side of the 'nose', start to needle felt the edges of the fibres in place.

4. Once the edges are secured, needle felt the rest of the fibres in place, from the nose tip to the top of the head. Fan out the top ends of the fibres, to create the natural shape of the head and help the nose fibres blend in with those of the base fur.

The finished nose. See how the vertical placement of the fibres has naturally created a bridge and tip of the nose?

ADDING DETAILS

By adding details, not only will you bring your animal to life, you can add personalized touches – whether it is a change in eye colour, the selection of markings or the expression. When adding details I recommend using a finer gauge felting needle, such as a 38 or 40. A larger gauge needle, whilst being more robust, may leave a rougher surface texture and can be harder to work into the fibres.

DETAILED EYES

More detailed eyes, such as the cat eye here, have been created by layering different-sized, different-coloured balls on top of each other. I usually use three colours – black for the base and pupil, a coloured fibre for the main eye colour and white for the glint. When needling into position, use the needle to slightly pull the edges of the bottom- and top-layer balls outwards to stretch them into ovals. This creates a more realistic eye shape.

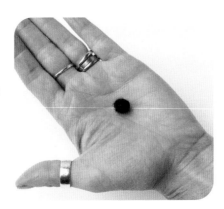

1. Pull off a small amount of fibres and roll them into a pea-sized ball.

2. Poke the ball into the eye socket with the needle-felting needle, then needle felt into place until it is flat. Make sure to pull out the corner of the ball with the needle to manipulate and shape the fibres to create a point at each end.

3. Take a smaller ball of coloured fibres and centre this over the felted black eye shape. Needle felt in place until it is flat. There's no need to shape this ball, as you want to keep it circular.

4. Needle felt flat a smaller black ball over the coloured fibres. Depending on the animal, this can be kept circular or stretched slightly at the top and bottom, as I have done here for the cat.

5. To finish, roll a very tiny white ball of fibres and needle felt it flat over the previous layer to make an eye glint – I have centred mine here for a focused gaze, but you could have it slightly off centre for a different look.

SIMPLE EYES

Simple eyes can be made by rolling a ball of felting fibres, (wool tops or roving) between your finger and thumb. This can then be carefully positioned and needled into place until it lies flat against the head.

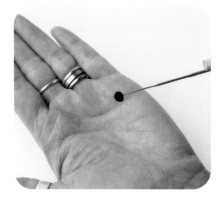

1. Pull off a tiny amount of black fibres and roll them into a ball with your finger and thumb.

2. Poke the ball into the eye socket with the needle-felting needle, then needle felt into place – start around the outer edge then work towards the centre.

EYEBROWS

Adding eyebrows can help to soften the eyes more, and add further structure and realism to the eye socket area.

1. Pull off a small amount of fibres that match the animal's fur and roll them into a small cocktail-sausage shape. Lay it over the face, one end by the bottom of the nose sculpted earlier then around the eye socket.

2. Needle felt in place.

3. Adding and felting a very fine amount of a paler colour on top, just above the eye, softens the eyebrow and creates a more natural effect too.

SIMPLE NOSE

Simple noses are created by rolling the wool tops or roving into a small ball and attaching them as shown here for Crunch the Mouse (see page 60), or by rolling them into two smaller balls for nostrils, as seen on Jellybean the Piglet (see page 106).

SHAPED NOSE

A shaped nose can be created for animals that suit a little more detail, like Marmalade the Cat (see page 120), Pickle the Dachshund (see page 66), Savanna the Lion (see page 98) or Twiglet the Koala (see page 114).

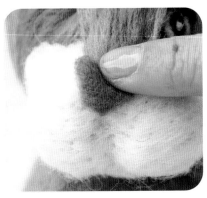

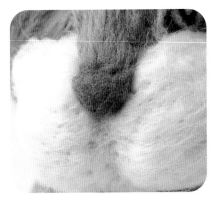

1. Pull off a small amount of fibres and form a shape with them like a triangle. Invert the shape and press it again the animal's face.

2. Attach along the top edge first then anchor the bottom point and shape the sides before needling in the middle of the shape. Any other detail can then be added on top of this shape as required.

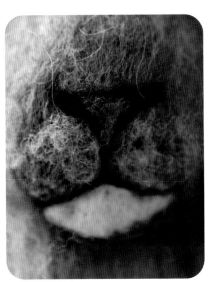

Left
Two different-sized, different-coloured triangles are layered here, pulled at the bottom to stretch the nose towards the mouth.

Right
Make a sideways oval with the nose, instead of a triangle, then add tiny balls of fibres for nostrils over the top.

LINEAR DETAILS

This technique is used for lots of details, from simple mouths to eye highlights. Think of this method like you're drawing with the fibres.

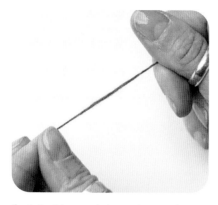

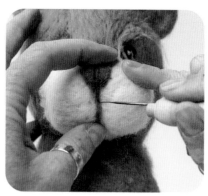

1. Pull a thin strand of your chosen colour and twist it into a line shape.

2. Lay this shape into position and hold down with your finger and thumb. Needle felt along the line where you want your line to be. Snip off any excess fibre and needle the ends until they disappear into the form.

3. If you are making a mouth, use the snipped excess or lengths of smaller fibres, and repeat steps 1 and 2 to make the 'curve' of the mouth to the left and right of the centre section.

INNER EARS

Make sure to use your foam block or rice bag/sock as a base to work on for this, to protect your hands. For ease, you could add details to the ears before they are sewn on at Stage 4.

WHAT TO DO: To add the colour within the inner ear, simply make a triangle with a thin length of your chosen colour of fibre then needle felt to the inside of the ear until flat.

> **- TIP -**
> *Some animals (like the koala and mice) have their inner ears knitted and sewn to the ear, before wet felting. This is because these inner ears are distinguished parts of the animals, and require a more secure attachment.*

FURRY TAIL

Some animals have a tufty end to the tail; others have 'full-on' fuzz all over their tails – this page shows you how to achieve both.

1. Pull off an 8cm (3in) length of 4cm (1½in) wide fibres, in your chosen colour. Lay them underneath the tail, with the end of the tail sitting centrally over the fibres.

2. Wrap the edges of the fibres around the end of the tail and pinch them in place.

3. Carefully needle felt across the middle of the wrapped fibres to partly secure them in position.

4. Continue to secure the fibres all the way around the tail.

5. Pull the tail end of the fibres upwards, enclosing the loose fibres. Pinch the two sections together.

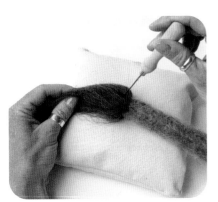 

6. Anchor in place by needle felting all around the base.

7. To finish, trim off any excess length with scissors, then thin the ends of the tail fur with the needle-felting needle.

- TIP -
The raccoon tail is made in exactly the same way, but with different coloured fibres added all the way up the shaft of the tail.

SEWING ON TOES

This is a technique used on 'toed' animals such as the lion, alpacas, cat and dachshund. You will need a tapestry needle and your chosen colour of knitting yarn – I tend to use black or dark brown for toes.

> **- TIP -**
> *It's easier to add your toes before sewing the animal together (see pages 36 and 37).*

1. Cut a 70cm (27½in) length of yarn and thread it onto your needle. About 2cm (¾in) down from the end of the foot or paw, and to one side, take the needle through the foot to the other side. Make a tiny anchor stitch, then bring the needle over the edge of the foot.

2. On the other side of the foot, take the needle down through the foot again – this time, enter the foot at a slight angle so that the tip of needle comes out 1cm (⅜in) or so next to the first stitched line.

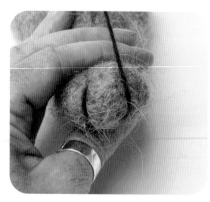

3. Pull the yarn tight to secure the first toe, and begin the second.

4. As in step 1, bring the needle over the edge of the foot to continue stitching the second toe.

5. As in step 2, take the needle through the foot at a slight angle, so that it comes out next to second toe and begins the third toe. Pull the yarn tight to secure the second toe.

6. Repeat the process in steps 1 and 2 to make the third and final toe.

7. To fasten off the yarn, make a small anchor stitch on the sole of the foot, over the third toe, then take the needle through the limb. Cut the yarn flush to finish.

The finished paw.

WHISKERS

Using a length of nylon fishing wire, add that final bit of realism and character to creatures such as Pebble the Seal (see page 90), Marmalade the Cat (see page 120) and Crunch the Mouse (see page 60).

1. Thread a 60cm (23½in) length of nylon fishing wire onto a tapestry needle. Holding the needle horizontally, take it through the cheek section of the animal, from one side to the other.

2. Pull until the end of the wire is hanging approximately 5cm (2in) out from the cheek.

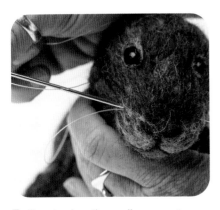

3. Close to where the needle came out, take the needle back through the cheek at a slight angle.

4. Bring the needle out the other side, just above the spot where the first whisker sits.

5. Cut the second whisker to the same length as the first.

6. Repeat the process once again on the right side of the face, then twice on the other side to finish.

> ❶ **WARNING** ❶
> *Do not add whiskers if the animal is intended for a small child.*

THE PROJECTS

Discover a variety of animals to knit and felt! Each animal has a difficulty level, so take the time to look through each project to make sure you're happy to tackle your chosen creature.

Most animals, depending on your experience and confidence, will take a few days to knit, and a few days to wet felt and needle felt.

For every creature you make, always read through the instructions carefully first, to make sure you have everything you need and you have an idea of what you need to do before you get started.

PEANUT & CRUNCH THE MICE

Peanut and Crunch are cheeky little friends who love to get into mischief together! They're so cute that you simply can't make one without the other – and since they're so easy to make, you don't need to choose! Peanut and Crunch will make a perfect weekend project.

Difficulty

• Easy

What you need

• Yarn

▷ 20g (¾oz) of Woolyknit Blue Faced Leicester in Iron, or equivalent DK (light worsted) weight 100% pure wool yarn in grey; 50g/113yd/102m *[A]*

▷ 10g (½oz) of Drops Puna in Powder Pink, or equivalent DK (light worsted) weight 100% pure wool yarn in dusky pink; 50g/120yd/110m *[B]*

• Felting fibres

▷ Natural-grey, steel-grey, coral and black merino wool tops

• Toy filling

Needles

• One pair of 4mm (UK 8; US 6) needles
• Tapestry needle
• Set of three needle-felting needles in sizes 40, 38 and 32

Tension/gauge

• 22 sts x 28 rows in a 10cm (4in) square over St st, using 4mm (UK 8; US 6) needles

INSTRUCTIONS

STAGE 1: THE KNIT BIT

Peanut (star-gazing mouse)

BODY & HEAD:
Using 4mm (UK 8; US 6) needles and yarn A, cast on 28 sts.
Row 1 (WS): purl.
Row 2: (k1, kfb) fourteen times (42 sts).
Rows 3–5: St st.
Row 6: (k2, k2tog) ten times, k2 (32 sts).
Rows 7–11: St st.
Row 12: (k2, k2tog) eight times (24 sts).
Rows 13–15: St st.
Row 16: (k2, k2tog) six times (18 sts).
Row 17: purl.
Row 18: (k2, k2tog) four times, k2 (14 sts).
Row 19: purl.
Row 20: (k2, k2tog) three times, k2 (11 sts).
Row 21: purl.
Row 22: k2, k2tog, k2, k2tog, k3 (9 sts).
Row 23: purl.
Row 24: (k1, k2tog) three times (6 sts).
Row 25: purl.
Row 26: (k1, k2tog) two times (4 sts).
Break yarn and thread through rem sts, pull tight and fasten off securely.

BASE:
Using 4mm (UK 8; US 6) needles and yarn A, cast on 6 sts.
Row 1 (WS): purl.
Row 2: kfb, k4, kfb (8 sts).
Rows 3–5: St st.
Row 6: k2tog, k4, k2tog (6 sts).
Row 7: purl.
Cast/bind off.

OUTER EAR (make two):
Using 4mm (UK 8; US 6) needles and yarn A, cast on 6 sts.
Row 1 (WS): purl.
Row 2: kfb, k4, kfb (8 sts).
Rows 3–5: St st.
Row 6: k2tog, k4, k2tog (6 sts).
Row 7: purl.
Cast/bind off.

INNER EAR (make two):
Using 4mm (UK 8; US 6) needles and yarn B, cast on 4 sts.
Row 1 (WS): purl.
Row 2: kfb, k2, kfb (6 sts).
Row 3: purl.
Row 4: k2tog, k2, k2tog (4 sts).
Row 5: purl.
Row 6: (k2tog) two times (2 sts).
Break yarn and thread through rem sts, pull tight and fasten off securely.

PAW (make four):
Using 4mm (UK 8; US 6) needles and yarn B, cast on 5 sts.
Row 1 (WS): purl.
Row 2: k2tog, k1, k2tog (3 sts).
Row 3: purl.
Break yarn and thread through rem sts, pull tight and fasten off securely.

TAIL:
Cut a 30cm (12in) length from yarn A and set aside until felting stage.

Crunch (scurrying mouse)

BODY & HEAD:
Using 4mm (UK 8; US 6) needles and yarn A, cast on 4 sts.
Row 1 (RS): (kfb) four times (8 sts).
Row 2: purl.
Row 3: (k1, kfb) four times (12 sts).
Row 4: purl.
Row 5: (k2, kfb) four times (16 sts).
Row 6: purl.
Row 7: (k3, kfb) four times (20 sts).
Row 8: purl.
Row 9: (k4, kfb) four times (24 sts).
Row 10: purl.
Row 11: (k5, kfb) four times (28 sts).
Rows 12–14: St st.
Row 15: (k2, kfb) nine times, k1 (37 sts).
Row 16: purl.
Row 17: (k6, kfb) five times, k2 (42 sts).
Rows 18–22: St st.
Row 23: (k6, k2tog) five times, k2 (37 sts).
Row 24: purl.
Row 25: (k5, k2tog) five times, k2 (32 sts).
Row 26: purl.
Row 27: (k4, k2tog) five times, k2 (27 sts).
Row 28: purl.
Row 29: (k1, k2tog) nine times (18 sts).
Row 30: purl.
Row 31: (k2tog) nine times (9 sts).
Break yarn and thread through rem sts, pull tight and fasten off securely.

OUTER EAR (make two):
Follow pattern for Peanut.

INNER EAR (make two):
Follow pattern for Peanut.

PAW (make four):
Follow pattern for Peanut.

TAIL:
Cut a 30cm (12in) length from yarn A and set aside until felting stage.

STAGE 2: SEWING UP

Peanut (star-gazing mouse)

1. With right sides together, sew together the row ends of the body from point to base with yarn A, leaving the cast-on edge open for stuffing later.

2. Sew the inner ear to the centre of the outer ear with yarn B, wrong sides facing.

3. Fold the 30cm (12in) length of yarn for the tail into thirds.

4. Fasten in all loose ends, as these can get in the way of wet felting later. Turn the hollow pieces the right side out.

Crunch (scurrying mouse)

5. With right sides facing, sew together the row ends of the body with yarn A, leaving a 2–3cm (¾–1in) space in the middle for stuffing into later.

6. Prepare the ears and tail in the same way as Peanut, in steps 2 and 4.

7. Fasten in all loose ends, as these can get in the way of wet felting later. Turn the hollow pieces the right side out.

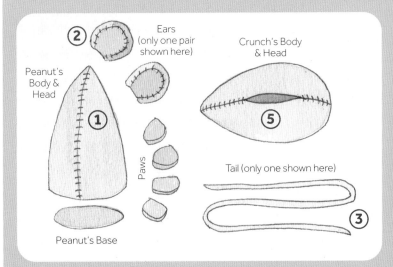

STAGE 3: WET FELTING

1. Wet felt the bodies for each mouse, following the wet felting information on page 31.

2. Wet felt the back of the sewn-together ears only and the little pink paws, following the information on page 31. With the feet, apply a little more pressure between finger and thumb until the knitted stitches blend together.

3. Briefly dip the folded tails in the water then roll the folded yarn between the palms of your hands until the three strands become one, thicker tail.

4. When all the pieces are felted equally, rinse them off. Pull all the flat pieces into shape; the remaining hollow pieces can be stuffed with kitchen roll.

5. Leave all the pieces to dry completely.

STAGE 4: STUFFING & CONSTRUCTION

Peanut (star-gazing mouse)

Stuff the body with toy filling and sew the base onto the bottom using yarn B. As you sew the last few stitches, you can add more stuffing to the base to make it firm. Push the base flat so that he stands up.

Crunch (scurrying mouse)

Stuff the body firmly and sew up the gap.

NOTE: The ears, paws and tails for both mice will be attached after the needle-felted fur has been added to the bodies.

STAGE 5: NEEDLE FELTING & DETAILS

1. Add a base layer of flat fur to both mice, following the instructions on page 39 and using natural-grey merino wool tops. Do not cover the cover the base of Peanut. Fluff up the fur on both bodies with the needle-felting needle, as described on page 41.

2. Pin the ears for each mouse into position then sew them in place with yarn A.

3. Pin the tail for each mouse into position. Sew them in place with yarn A.

4. Pin the paws onto the body for each mouse, using the diagram above to help you. Sew them in place with yarn B.

5. Make simple eyes for your mouse with black merino wool tops, following the instructions on page 52.

6. Make simple noses for both mice with the coral merino wool tops, following the information on page 53.

7. 'Draw' the lines of the mouths of both mice with twisted steel-grey merino wool tops, following the Linear Details instructions on page 54. Add a little open mouth by rolling a tiny ball with the coral merino wool tops, then needle felt this just below the upside-down 'V' of the twisted steel-grey fibres.

65

PICKLE THE DACHSHUND

Pickle is a handsome little chap who's full of fun, and is an impressive-looking animal to make. Pickle is knitted using aran (worsted) weight yarn, so he grows quite quickly (the thicker the yarn, the quicker the item is knitted!). Although he is a combination of simple shapes, there are a few extra limbs to sew together, so a little forethought may be needed at Stage 4. However, all your efforts are worth it – once they're all joined together, this is a project with the wow factor!

Difficulty

• Intermediate

What you need

• Yarn
▷ *110g (¾oz) of Woolyknit Aran in Pirate Grey, or equivalent aran (worsted) weight 100% pure wool yarn in dark grey; 50g/85yd/77m [A]*
▷ *Small amount of black yarn, for the paws*

• Felting fibres
▷ *Tan, white, dark-brown and black merino wool tops*

• Toy filling

• Stitch marker (a contrasting-coloured scrap of yarn makes a handy, economical alternative)

Needles

• One pair of 5mm (UK 6; US 8) needles
• Tapestry needle
• Set of three needle-felting needles in sizes 40, 38 and 32

Tension/gauge

• 28 sts x 24 rows in a 10cm (4in) square over St st, using 5mm (UK 6; US 8) needles

INSTRUCTIONS

STAGE 1: THE KNIT BIT

BODY:

Using 5mm (UK 6; US 8) needles, cast on 6 sts in yarn A.

Row 1 (RS): (kfb) six times (12 sts).
Row 2: purl.
Row 3: (k1, kfb) six times (18 sts).
Row 4: purl.
Row 5: (k2, kfb) six times (24 sts).
Row 6: purl.
Row 7: (k3, kfb) six times (30 sts).
Row 8: purl.
Row 9: (k4, kfb) six times (36 sts).
Rows 10-34: St st.
Row 35: (k5, kfb) six times (42 sts).
Rows 36-44: St st.
Row 45: (k6, kfb) six times (48 sts).
Rows 46-56: St st.
Row 57: (k6, k2tog) six times (42 sts).
Row 58: purl.
Row 59: (k5, k2tog) six times (36 sts).

Row 60: purl.
Row 61: (k4, k2tog) six times (30 sts).
Row 62: purl.
Row 63: (k3, k2tog) six times (24 sts).
Row 64: purl.
Row 65: (k2, k2tog) six times (18 sts).
Row 66: purl.
Row 67: (k1, k2tog) six times (12 sts).
Row 68: purl.
Row 69: (k2tog) six times (6 sts).
Break yarn and thread through rem sts, pull tight and fasten off securely.

HEAD:

Using 5mm (UK 6; US 8) needles, cast on 16 sts in yarn A.

Row 1 (WS): purl.
Row 2: kfb, k14, kfb (18 sts).
Row 3: purl.
Row 4: kfb, k16, kfb (20 sts).
Row 5: purl.

Row 6: (k4, kfb) four times (24 sts).
Row 7: purl.
Row 8: (k5, kfb) four times (28 sts).
Row 9: purl.
Row 10: (k6, kfb) four times (32 sts).
Row 11: purl.
Row 12: kfb, k30, kfb (34 sts). Place a stitch marker here.
Rows 13-19: St st starting with a p row.
Row 20: k2tog, k30, k2tog (32 sts).
Row 21: purl.
Row 22: (k6, k2tog) four times (28 sts).
Row 23: purl.
Row 24: (k5, k2tog) four times (24 sts).
Row 25: purl.
Row 26: (k4, k2tog) four times (20 sts).
Row 27: purl.
Row 28: (k3, k2tog) four times (16 sts).
Row 29: purl.
Row 30: (k2tog) eight times (8 sts).
Break yarn and thread through rem sts, pull tight and fasten off securely.

MUZZLE:

Using 5mm (UK 6; US 8) needles, cast on 8 sts in yarn A.

Row 1 (WS): purl.
Row 2: kfb, k6, kfb (10 sts).
Row 3: purl.
Row 4: kfb, k8, kfb (12 sts).
Row 5: purl.
Row 6: kfb, k10, kfb (14 sts).
Row 7: purl.
Row 8: kfb, k12, kfb (16 sts).
Rows 9-11: St st.
Row 12: (k3, kfb) four times (20 sts).
Rows 13-15: St st.
Row 16: (k4, kfb) four times (24 sts).
Row 17: purl.
Cast/bind off.

RIGHT EAR:

Using 5mm (UK 6; US 8) needles, cast on 4 sts in yarn A.

Row 1 (WS): purl.
Row 2: kfb, k2, kfb (6 sts).
Row 3: purl.
Row 4: k5, kfb (7 sts).
Row 5: purl.
Row 6: k6, kfb (8 sts).
Row 7: purl.
Row 8: k7, kfb (9 sts).
Row 9: purl.
Row 10: k8, kfb (10 sts).
Row 11: purl.
Row 12: k9, kfb (11 sts).
Rows 13-15: St st starting with a p row.
Row 16: k10, kfb (12 sts).
Row 17: purl.
Row 18: k11, kfb (13 sts).
Row 19: purl.
Row 20: cast off 2 sts, k to last st, kfb (12 sts).
Row 21: purl.
Row 22: cast off 2 sts, k to last st, kfb (11 sts).
Row 23: purl.
Cast/bind off.

LEFT EAR:

Using 5mm (UK 6; US 8) needles, cast on 4 sts in yarn A.

Row 1 (WS): purl.
Row 2: kfb, k2, kfb (6 sts).
Row 3: purl.
Row 4: kfb, k5 (7 sts).
Row 5: purl.
Row 6: kfb, k6 (8 sts).
Row 7: purl.
Row 8: kfb, k7 (9 sts).
Row 9: purl.
Row 10: kfb, k8 (10 sts).
Row 11: purl.
Row 12: kfb, k9 (11 sts).
Rows 13-15: St st starting with a p row.
Row 16: kfb, k10 (12 sts).
Row 17: purl.
Row 18: kfb, k11 (13 sts).
Row 19: purl.
Row 20: kfb, k12 (14 sts).
Row 21: cast off 2 sts, p to end (12 sts)
Row 22: kfb, k11 (13 sts).
Row 23: cast off 2 sts, p to end (11 sts).
Cast/bind off.

RIGHT FRONT LEG:

Using 5mm (UK 6; US 8) needles, cast on 4 sts in yarn A.

Row 1 (WS): purl.
Row 2: kfb, k2, kfb (6 sts).
Row 3: purl.
Row 4: kfb, k4, kfb (8 sts).
Row 5: purl.
Row 6: cast on 8 sts, k to end (16 sts).
Rows 7-11: St st starting with a p row.
Row 12: k12, *turn*.
Row 13: p8, *turn*.
Row 14: k7, k2tog, *turn*.
Row 15: p7, p2tog, *turn*.
Rows 16-21: rep last 2 rows three times more (8 sts).
Rows 22-25: St st.
Row 26: k2tog, k4, k2tog (6 sts).
Row 27: p2tog, p2, p2tog (4 sts).
Row 28: (k2tog) twice (2 sts).
Row 29: purl.
Break yarn and thread through rem sts, pull tight and fasten off securely.

- TURNING YOUR KNITTING -

When you 'turn' your knitting, you are literally turning it part way through the row you are working on, before you have 'finished' the row. To continue you begin a new row, working only on the stitches you have knitted before the turn. This creates shape, and is something sock knitters use all the time.

LEFT FRONT LEG:

Using 5mm (US 6; US 8) needles, cast on 4 sts in yarn A.

Row 1 (RS): knit.
Row 2: purl.
Row 3: kfb, k2, kfb (6 sts).
Row 4: purl.
Row 5: kfb, k4, kfb (8 sts).
Row 6: cast on 8 sts, p to end (16 sts).
Rows 7–11: St st.
Row 12: p12, *turn*.
Row 13: k8, *turn*.
Row 14: p7, p2tog, *turn*.
Row 15: k7, k2tog, *turn*.
Rows 16–21: rep last 2 rows three times more (8 sts).
Rows 22–25: St st.
Row 26: p2tog, p4, p2tog (6 sts).
Row 27: k2tog, k2, k2tog (4 sts).
Row 28: (p2tog) twice (2 sts).
Break yarn and thread through rem sts, pull tight and fasten off securely.

REAR LEG – UPPER SECTION (make two):

Using 5mm (UK 6; US 8) needles, cast on 4 sts in yarn A.

Row 1 (RS): (kfb) four times (8 sts).
Row 2: purl.
Row 3: kfb, k6, kfb (10 sts).
Row 4: purl.
Row 5: kfb, k8, kfb (12 sts).
Row 6: purl.
Row 7: kfb, k10, kfb (14 sts).
Row 8: purl.
Row 9: kfb, k12, kfb (16 sts).
Row 10: purl.
Row 11: cast on 8 sts, k to end (24 sts).
Row 12: cast on 8 sts, p to end (32 sts).
Row 13: k6, (k2tog) twice, k12, (k2tog) twice, k6 (28 sts).
Row 14: purl.
Row 15: k5, (k2tog) twice, k10, (k2tog) twice, k5 (24 sts).
Row 16: purl.
Row 17: (k2, k2tog) six times (18 sts).
Row 18: purl.
Row 19: (k1, k2tog) six times (12 sts).
Rows 20–22: St st.
Row 23: (k2tog) six times (6 sts).
Break yarn and thread through rem sts, pull tight and fasten off securely.

REAR LEG – LOWER SECTION (make two):

Using 5mm (UK 6; US 8) needles, cast on 12 sts in yarn A.

Rows 1 (WS)–3: St st starting with a p row.
Row 4: k9, *turn*.
Row 5: p6, *turn*.
Row 6: k5, k2tog, *turn*.
Row 7: p5, p2tog, *turn*.
Rows 8–11: rep last 2 rows twice more (6 sts).
Rows 12–15: St st.
Row 16: k2tog, k2, k2tog (4 sts).
Row 17: purl.
Row 18: (k2tog) twice (2 sts).
Break yarn and thread through rem sts, pull tight and secure.

TAIL:

Using 5mm (UK 6; US 8) needles, cast on 12 sts in yarn A.

Rows 1 (WS)–7: St st starting with a p row.
Row 8: k2tog, k8, k2tog (10 sts).
Rows 9–15: St st starting with a p row.
Row 16: k2tog, k6, k2tog (8 sts).
Rows 17–23: St st starting with a p row.
Row 24: k2tog, k4, k2tog (6 sts).
Rows 25–27: St st starting with a p row.
Row 28: (k2tog) three times (3 sts).
Break yarn and thread through rem sts, pull tight and fasten off securely.

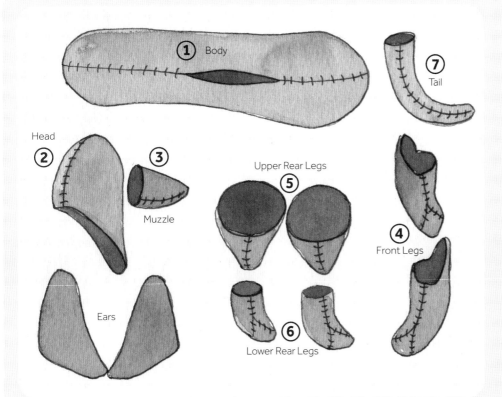

STAGE 2: SEWING UP

1. With right sides facing, sew together the row ends of the body with yarn A, leaving a 4–5cm (1½–2in) stuffing gap in the middle for stuffing into later.

2. With the right sides facing, sew up the row ends of the head with yarn A, starting from the top of the head and working down to the stitch marker.

3. With the right sides facing, sew together the row ends of the muzzle with yarn A, leaving the cast-on edge open for stuffing later.

4. With the right sides facing, sew up the left and right front legs with yarn A, using the diagram above and the instructions on page 26 to help you: fold the leg in half from the point of the toe, turn in the toe and sew up the length of the leg and each side of the foot as indicated. (Note: one side of the leg will be taller than the other.)

5. With right sides facing, sew together the bottom part of the upper rear legs with yarn A, up to where the extra stitches were cast on. This creates little funnel-like shapes.

6. With the right sides facing, sew up the lower rear legs, using the diagram above and the instructions on page 26 to help you: fold the leg in half from the point of the toe, turn in the toe and sew up the length of the leg and each side of the foot as indicated.

7. With right sides facing, sew together the row ends of the tail with yarn A, working towards the point and leaving the cast-on edge open for stuffing into later. Leave the yarn attached, then use this to sew a long running stitch back up the seam. Pull the tail of yarn to make the tail curl (see photo detail, opposite).

8. Fasten in all loose ends, as these can get in the way of wet felting later. Turn the hollow pieces right side out.

STAGE 3: WET FELTING

1. Wet felt all the pieces of Pickle, following the wet felting information on pages 30 and 31.

2. When all the pieces are felted equally, rinse them all off. Pull the ears into shape. The remaining hollow pieces can be stuffed with kitchen roll.

3. Leave all the pieces to dry completely.

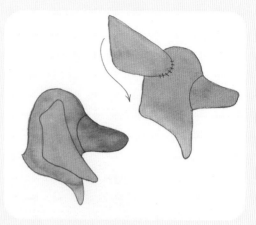

STAGE 4: STUFFING & CONSTRUCTION

1. Stuff the body firmly and sew up the space left in the tummy with yarn A.

2. Stuff the head and pin it into position, referring to the diagram above. When you are happy with your positioning, sew the head to the body with yarn A using small, close stitches. Add extra stuffing before completely sewing on the head, if required.

3. Position and pin the muzzle onto the head (the seam should be facing down). When you are happy with your positioning, sew the muzzle in place with yarn A, using small, close stitches. Add extra stuffing before completely sewing on the muzzle, if required.

4. Stuff the lower rear legs and pin them into position onto the upper rear legs, as shown in the diagram. Sew them in place with yarn A.

5. Pin the tops of the upper rear legs onto each side of the body, towards the back, as shown in the diagram. Sew them in place with yarn A. Add extra stuffing before completely sewing them on, if required.

6. Stuff the front legs then pin them onto each side of the body, towards the front, as shown in the diagram. Note that the shape of the legs should match the shape of the body. Sew them in place with yarn A. Add extra stuffing before completely sewing them on, if required.

NOTE: The ears will be attached after the base layer of black merino wool tops has been needle felted to the body.

STAGE 5: NEEDLE FELTING & DETAILS

1. I really wanted to create the smooth, glossy look of a dachshund with this design, so I decided to add a nice base layer of black merino wool tops. Follow the instructions for flat fur on page 39 to add a base layer of black merino all over the body. When adding the fur to the tail and ears, use a foam block or rice bag to protect your fingers and work surface.

2. Use the tan merino wool tops to add smooth patches of colour to the muzzle, tummy, chest and paws, following the flat fur instructions on page 39 and using the photographs to help you.

3. To attach the ears, sew them to the head as shown in the top right-hand diagram, opposite, then fold them down to the sides of the head and secure with a few small stitches under each ear. (The longest point of the ear is to the front).

4. Make the detailed eyes for Pickle, using the instructions on page 51 as a guide: the order of merino wool tops colours, from base to top, is dark-brown, black then white.

5. To finish the eyes and add further definition, twist two fine lengths of white merino wool tops and needle felt one to the bottom of each eye, using the Linear Details technique on page 54.

6. Sculpt eyebrows for Pickle with the tan merino wool tops, following the instructions on page 52.

7. Make a shaped nose for Pickle with the black merino wool tops, following the instructions on page 53.

8. 'Draw' the lines of the mouth with twisted black merino wool tops, following the Linear Details technique on page 54.

9. Using some of your black yarn, sew toes onto each paw, following the instructions on page 56.

COCOA & WAFFLE
THE ALPACAS

Not only do these guys have the cutest faces, they are so easy to make, too! The body and legs are knitted in one piece, so they are nice and strong, and there are only a few pieces to sew together. Both the alpacas are made in exactly the same way; the only differences are the yarn and fibre colours! Why not customize your design, and make them in a variety of colours or with different fur types?

Difficulty

• Easy

What you need

• Yarn
▷ 90g (3¼oz) of Drops Alaska in Beige **OR** Off White, or equivalent aran (worsted) weight 100% pure wool yarn in walnut-brown or cream 50g/77yd/70m **[A]**
▷ Small amount of black **OR** dark-grey yarn, for the hoof detail

• Felting fibres
▷ Mid-brown **OR** natural white fleece
▷ Mid-brown **OR** white wool roving
▷ Black **OR** dark-grey and white merino wool tops

• Toy filling

• Stitch marker (a contrasting-coloured scrap of yarn makes a handy, economical alternative)

Needles

• One pair of 5mm (UK 6; US 8) needles
• Tapestry needle
• Set of three needle-felting needles in sizes 40, 38 and 32

Tension/gauge

• 17 sts x 22 rows in a 10cm (4in) square over St st, using 5mm (UK 6; US 8) needles

INSTRUCTIONS

STAGE 1: THE KNIT BIT

BODY:

Using 5mm (UK 6; US 8) needles, cast on 60 sts in yarn A.

Rows 1 (WS)-13: St st starting with a p row.
Row 14: cast off 14 sts, k to end (46 sts).
Row 15: cast off 14 sts, p to end (32 sts).
Rows 16 and 17: St st.
Row 18: k1, kfb, k28, kfb, k1 (34 sts).
Rows 19-23: St st starting with a p row.
Row 24: k1, kfb, k30, kfb, k1 (36 sts).
Rows 25-31: St st starting with a p row.
Row 32: k2tog, k32, k2tog (34 sts).
Rows 33-39: St st starting with a p row.
Row 40: cast on 5 sts, k to end (39 sts).
Row 41: cast on 5 sts, p to end (44 sts).
Row 42: k1, kfb, k40, kfb, k1 (46 sts).
Rows 43: purl.
Row 44: k1, kfb, k42, kfb, k1 (48 sts).
Row 45: purl.
Row 46: k1, kfb, k44, kfb, k1 (50 sts).
Row 47: cast on 5 sts, p to end (55 sts).
Row 48: cast on 5 sts, k to end (60 sts).
Rows 49-60: St st starting with a p row. Cast/bind off.

HEAD & NECK:

Using 5mm (UK 6; US 8) needles, cast on 3 sts in yarn A.

Row 1 (WS): purl.
Row 2: kfb, k1, kfb (5 sts).
Row 3: purl.
Row 4: kfb, k3, kfb (7 sts).
Row 5: purl.
Row 6: kfb, k5, kfb (9 sts).
Row 7: purl.
Row 8: kfb, k7, kfb (11 sts).
Rows 9-11: St st starting with a p row.
Row 12: cast on 3 sts, k to end (14 sts). Place a stitch marker here.
Row 13: cast on 3 sts, p to end (17 sts).
Row 14: kfb, k15, kfb (19 sts).
Rows 15-25: St st starting with a p row.
Row 26: k1, k2tog, k13, k2tog, k1 (17 sts).
Row 27: purl.
Row 28: k1, k2tog, k11, k2tog, k1 (15 sts).

Row 29: purl.
Row 30: (k1, k2tog) five times (10 sts). Break yarn and thread through rem sts, pull tight and fasten off securely.

TUMMY:

Using 5mm (UK 6; US 8) needles, cast on 14 sts in yarn A.

Row 1 (WS): purl.
Row 2: kfb, k12, kfb (16 sts).
Row 3: purl.

Row 4: kfb, k14, kfb (18 sts).
Row 5: purl.
Row 6: kfb, k16, kfb (20 sts).
Row 7: purl.
Row 8: kfb, k18, kfb (22 sts).
Row 9: purl.
Row 10: k2tog, k18, k2tog (20 sts).
Row 11: purl.
Row 12: k2tog, k16, k2tog (18 sts).
Row 13: purl.
Row 14: k2tog, k14, k2tog (16 sts).

Row 15: purl.
Row 16: k2tog, k12, k2tog (14 sts).
Row 17: purl.
Cast/bind off.

EAR (make two):
Using 5mm (UK 6; US 8) needles, cast on 7 sts in yarn A.
Row 1 (WS): purl.
Cast/bind off.

MUZZLE:
Using 5mm (UK 6; US 8) needles, cast on 15 sts in yarn A.
Rows 1 (WS)–3: St st starting with a p row.
Row 4: (k1, k2tog) five times (10 sts).
Rows 5–7: St st starting with a p row.
Row 8: (k2tog) five times (5 sts).
Break yarn and thread through rem sts, pull tight and fasten off securely.

STAGE 2: SEWING UP

1. With right sides facing and referring to the diagram right, sew up the legs on the all-in-one body with yarn A. Once the legs are sewn together, pinch points A and B together then pin in place. Repeat with points C and D. Sew each pinched together section in place, following the instructions on page 23.

2. Still with right sides facing, stitch across each corner at the front and back of the body, at the places indicated by the 'X' on the diagram, using yarn A. Doing this means that when it is turned the right way out, the body forms a rounded shape.

3. With the right sides facing, sew up the row ends of the head & neck, starting from the top of the head then down to the marker.

4. Sew up the row ends of the muzzle, leaving the cast-on edge open for stuffing into later.

5. Fasten in all loose ends before wet felting, as these can get in the way. Turn all the hollow pieces the right way out.

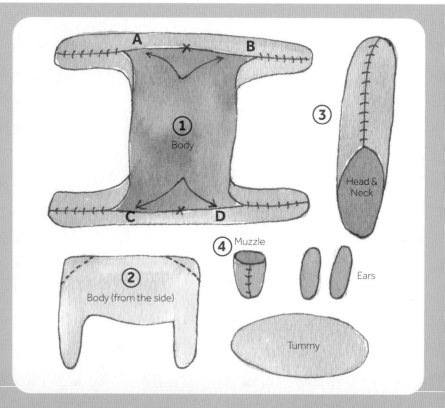

① Body

③ Head & Neck

④ Muzzle

Ears

② Body (from the side)

Tummy

STAGE 3: WET FELTING

1. Wet felt the body, head & neck and tummy of the alpaca, following the information on page 30.

2. Wet felt the ears and muzzle, following the information on page 31.

3. When all the pieces are felted equally, rinse them off. Pull the ears and tummy pieces into shape – the ears should be slightly curved and concave. The remaining hollow pieces can be stuffed with kitchen roll.

4. Leave all the pieces to dry completely.

STAGE 4: STUFFING & CONSTRUCTION

1. Stuff the all-in-one body firmly then pin the tummy piece into position over the stuffing gap. Sew the tummy in place with yarn A, adding extra stuffing before closing up completely to make a nice, rounded belly.

2. Stuff the head & neck and pin it into position, referring to the diagram below. When you are happy with your positioning, sew the head & neck to the body with yarn A using small, close stitches. Add extra stuffing before completely closing up, especially down the front of the neck, to make it nice and plump.

3. Stuff the muzzle then pin it onto the front of the head – the seam edge should be facing down. When you are happy with your positioning, sew the muzzle in place with yarn A using small, close stitches.

4. Position and pin the ears. When you are happy with your positioning, sew the base of the ears to the head with yarn A using small, close stitches.

STAGE 5: NEEDLE FELTING & DETAILS

NOTE (IF YOU ARE MAKING THE WHITE ALPACA): When felting white or cream yarn, it is often difficult to felt out all traces of the knitted stitches completely. This is sometimes due to the process that the yarn has gone through to make it pale in colour. In these cases, I recommend covering exposed areas of stitching, such as the ankles and face of the alpaca, with a thin layer of natural fleece or cream wool roving until any visible knitted stitches are hidden.

1. Cover the feet, face and ears of the alpacas with a thin layer of mid-brown or white wool roving, following the instructions for laying flat fur on page 39.

2. Following the instructions on page 40, add a layer of mid-brown or natural white fleece or wool roving two-thirds of the way down each leg, all over the body, the neck and up to the top of the head, leaving the face, ears and feet untouched.

3. Add a thin layer of mid-brown or white wool roving to the inner ears, following the instructions on page 54.

4. Make a tail by rolling a small, firm sausage shape from mid-brown or white wool roving and needle felting it to the back of the body. Needle felt around the edges first to establish the shape, then lightly needle felt from the top to the middle of the tail, scattering the needling the further down you go, so that the end of the tail remains proud.

5. Sculpt the bridge of the nose: needle down each side of the nose in a line, without any fibre – this will push in the shape of the knitting and create a ridge along each side of the nose (see photo detail, bottom left).

6. Make tiny detailed eyes for your alpaca, using the information on page 51 as a guide: the order of merino wool tops colours, from base to top, is black (if you are making Cocoa) or dark-grey (if you are making Waffle), then white (for both).

7. Following the instructions on page 52, use the mid-brown or white roving to sculpt eyebrows for your alpaca.

8. Roll two tiny balls with the black merino wool tops and needle felt them to the end of the muzzle to add nostrils – apply the stretching technique described in step 2 of the Detailed Eyes technique on page 51, to shape them into slight ovals with your needle.

9. 'Draw' the lines of the mouth with twisted black merino wool tops, following the Linear Details technique on page 54.

10. Using black yarn if you are making Cocoa, or grey yarn if you are making Waffle, work two to three overstitches through the end of each foot to create a toes. Fasten off the yarn, following the instructions on page 56.

DANDELION THE RABBIT

Dandelion is a sweet little bunny who loves to have cuddles and strokes!
You are sure to fall in love with this creation, as Dandelion is an ideal
project for the first-time knitter and felter. She is made with aran (worsted)
weight yarn (meaning she's quicker to knit), her knitting pattern is simple
to follow, and only a small amount of needle felting is required –
and will give great results!

Difficulty

• Easy

What you need

• Yarn

▷ 40g (1½oz) of Drops Nepal in Beige Mix, or equivalent aran (worsted) weight alpaca-
sheep wool-blend yarn in light, variegated beige; 50g/82yd/75m [A]
▷ Small amount of dark-brown yarn, for the toes

• Felting fibres

▷ White, black and slate-blue merino wool tops
▷ Mid-brown and beige wool roving
▷ Natural white fleece, for the tail

• Toy filling

Needles

• One pair of 5mm (UK 6; US 8) needles
• Tapestry needle
• Set of three needle-felting needles in sizes 40, 38 and 32

Tension/gauge

• 17 sts x 22 rows in a 10cm (4in) square over St st,
using 5mm (UK 6; US 8) needles

INSTRUCTIONS

STAGE 1: THE KNIT BIT

BODY:
Using 5mm (UK 6; US 8) needles, cast on 8 sts in yarn A.
Row 1 (RS): (kfb) in every st (16 sts).
Row 2: purl.
Row 3: (k1, kfb) eight times (24 sts).
Row 4: purl.
Row 5: (k2, kfb) eight times (32 sts).
Row 6: purl.
Row 7: (k3, kfb) eight times (40 sts).
Rows 8-14: St st.
Row 15: (k4, kfb) eight times (48 sts).
Rows 16-20: St st.
Row 21: (k4, k2tog) eight times (40 sts).
Row 22: purl.
Row 23: (k3, k2tog) eight times (32 sts).
Row 24: purl.
Row 25: (k2, k2tog) eight times (24 sts).
Row 26: purl.
Row 27: (k1, k2tog) eight times (16 sts).
Row 28: purl.
Row 29: (k2tog) eight times (8 sts).
Break yarn and thread through rem sts, pull tight and fasten off securely.

HEAD:
Using 5mm (UK 6; US 8) needles, cast on 4 sts in yarn A.
Row 1 (RS): (kfb) in every st (8 sts).
Row 2: purl.
Row 3: (k1, kfb) four times (12 sts).
Row 4: purl.
Row 5: (k2, kfb) four times (16 sts).
Row 6: purl.
Row 7: (k3, kfb) four times (20 sts).
Row 8: purl.
Row 9: (k4, kfb) four times (24 sts).
Rows 10-16: St st.
Row 17: (k4, k2tog) four times (20 sts).
Row 18: purl.
Row 19: (k3, k2tog) four times (16 sts).
Row 20: purl.
Row 21: (k2, k2tog) four times (12 sts).
Row 22: purl.

Row 23: (k1, k2tog) four times (8 sts).
Row 24: purl.
Row 25: (k2tog) four times (4 sts).
Break yarn and thread through rem sts, pull tight and fasten off securely.

EAR (make two):
Using 5mm (UK 6; US 8) needles, cast on 10 sts in yarn A.
Rows 1 (WS)-3: St st starting with a p row.
Row 4: kfb, k8, kfb (12 sts).
Rows 5-7: St st starting with a p row.
Row 8: kfb, k10, kfb (14 sts).
Rows 9-11: St st starting with a p row.
Row 12: k2tog, k10, k2tog (12 sts).
Row 13: purl.
Row 14: k2tog, k8, k2tog (10 sts).
Row 15: purl.
Row 16: k2tog, k6, k2tog (8 sts).
Row 17: purl.
Row 18: k2tog, k4, k2tog (6 sts).
Row 19: purl.
Row 20: k2tog, k2, k2tog (4 sts).
Break yarn and thread through rem sts, pull tight and secure.

FRONT PAW (make two):
Using 5mm (UK 6; US 8) needles, cast on 12 sts in yarn A.
Rows 1 (WS)-5: St st starting with a p row.
Row 6: (k2tog) six times (6 sts).
Break yarn and thread through rem sts, pull tight and fasten off securely.

STAGE 2: SEWING UP

1. With right sides facing, sew together the row ends of the body with yarn A, leaving a 4–5cm (1½–2in) gap in the middle for stuffing into later.

2. Fold in the top, flatter edges of the ears, wrong sides together, as shown in the diagram below. Secure the folds with a few stitches, using yarn A.

3. Fasten in the loose yarn ends of the head, creating an oval cupped shape.

4. Sew together the row ends of the front paws, leaving the cast-on edge open for stuffing.

5. Fasten in all remaining loose ends, before wet felting, as these can get in the way. Turn all pieces the right way out.

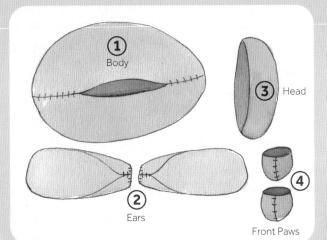

Body

Head ③

② Ears

④ Front Paws

STAGE 3: WET FELTING

1. Wet felt the body and head, following the information on page 30.

2. Wet felt the ears and paws, following the information on page 31.

3. When all the pieces are felted equally, rinse them all off. Pull the ears into shape; the remaining hollow pieces can be stuffed with kitchen roll.

4. Leave all the pieces to dry completely.

STAGE 4: STUFFING & CONSTRUCTION

1. Stuff the body firmly then sew up the gap with yarn A.

2. Stuff the head and pin it into position on the front of the body. When you are happy with your positioning, sew the head in place with yarn A using small, close stitches. Add extra stuffing before completely closing up, if required.

3. Stuff then pin the front paws onto the body, using the diagram below and the photograph on page 81 to help you. Once you are happy, sew them in place with yarn A.

4. Position the ears as shown in the diagram below and sew them to the top of the head, at each side, with yarn A. If the ears stick out too much, sew additional, tiny anchor stitches between the sides of the ears and the body to help them lay flat.

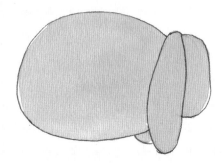

STAGE 5: NEEDLE FELTING & DETAILS

1. To make the tail, begin by rolling a golf ball-sized ball with the natural white fleece. Position it at the back of the body, then needle felt along the bottom edge by a few centimetres (an inch) or so. Pull the ball slightly on one side, so the fibres form an upside-down teardrop shape. Needle felt the tail in place, around the outer edges and only here and there in the middle, to help the tail stand proud. If necessary, needle felt a little more at the base so that it's flat against the body.

2. Make the detailed eyes for Dandelion, using the instructions on page 51 as a guide: the order of merino wool tops colours, from base to top, is slate-blue, black then white.

3. Needle felt some very fine layers of mid-brown wool roving and white merino tops here and there onto the nose section of the face, to add a little colour to the top of the nose.

4. 'Draw' the lines of the mouth with twisted black merino wool tops, following the Linear Details technique on page 54.

5. To make the tuft of hair on top of the head, pull off a thin amount of beige wool roving and roll it into a light ball. Needle felt it onto the top of the head here and there only, to keep the volume of the tuft!

6. Following the information on page 56, sew two toe indents onto each paw using the dark brown yarn.

ROCKY THE RACCOON

Rocky is a friendly little guy who promises to be good and not pinch your treats (now and then)! He is a great intermediate project, combining easy knitting techniques with a good variety of different needle-felting tasks to keep things interesting.

Difficulty

• Intermediate

What you need

• Yarn

▷ *50g (1¾oz) of Woolyknit Blue Faced Leicester in Iron, or equivalent DK (light worsted) weight 100% pure wool yarn in grey; 50g/113yd/102m [A]*

▷ *20g (1¾oz) of Drops Puna in Black, or equivalent DK (light worsted) weight 100% pure coarse wool yarn in charcoal; 50g/82yd/110m [B]*

• Felting fibres

▷ *White, steel-grey and black merino wool tops*
▷ *Grey wool roving*
▷ *Natural white fleece*

• Toy filling

• Stitch marker (a contrasting-coloured scrap of yarn makes a handy, economical alternative)

Needles

• One pair of 4mm (UK 8; US 6) needles
• Tapestry needle
• Set of three needle-felting needles in sizes 40, 38 and 32

Tension/gauge

• 22 sts x 28 rows in a 10cm (4in) square over St st, using 4mm (UK 8; US 6) needles

INSTRUCTIONS

STAGE 1: THE KNIT BIT

BODY:
Using 4mm (UK 8; US 6) needles, cast on 6 sts in yarn A.
Row 1 (WS): purl.
Row 2: (kfb) six times (12 sts).
Row 3: purl.
Row 4: (k1, kfb) six times (18 sts).
Row 5: purl.
Row 6: (k2, kfb) six times (24 sts).
Row 7: purl.
Row 8: (k3, kfb) six times (30 sts).
Row 9: purl.
Row 10: (k4, kfb) six times (36 sts).
Row 11: purl.
Row 12: (k5, kfb) six times (42 sts).
Row 13: purl.
Row 14: (k6, kfb) six times (48 sts).
Row 15: purl.
Row 16: (k7, kfb) six times (54 sts).
Rows 17-31: St st starting with a p row.
Row 32: (k7, k2tog) six times (48 sts).
Row 33: purl.
Row 34: (k6, k2tog) six times (42 sts).
Rows 35-37: St st starting with a p row.
Row 38: (k5, k2tog) six times (36 sts).
Row 39: purl.
Row 40: (k4, k2tog) six times (30 sts).
Row 41: purl.
Row 42: (k3, k2tog) six times (24 sts).
Row 43: purl.
Row 44: (k2, k2tog) six times (18 sts).
Row 45: purl.
Row 46: (k2tog) nine times (9 sts).
Break yarn and thread through rem sts, pull tight and fasten off securely.

HEAD:
Using 4mm (UK 8; US 6) needles, cast on 26 sts in yarn A.
Row 1 (WS): purl.
Row 2: kfb, k24, kfb (28 sts).
Row 3: purl.
Row 4: kfb, k26, kfb (30 sts).
Rows 5-9: St st starting with a p row.
Row 10: (k4, k2tog) five times (25 sts).
Row 11: purl.
Row 12: (k3, k2tog) five times (20 sts).
Row 13: purl.

Row 14: (k2, k2tog) five times (15 sts).
Row 15: purl.
Row 16: (k1, k2tog) five times (10 sts).
Row 17: purl.
Row 18: (k2tog) five times (5 sts).
Break yarn and thread through rem sts, pull tight and fasten off securely.

PAW (make four):
Using 4mm (UK 8; US 6) needles, cast on 10 sts in yarn B.
Rows 1 (WS)-3: St st starting with a p row.
Row 4: kfb, k8, kfb (12 sts).
Rows 5-7: St st starting with a p row.
Row 8: k2tog, k8, k2tog (10 sts).
Row 9: purl.
Row 10: (k2tog) five times (5 sts).
Break yarn and thread through rem sts, pull tight and fasten off securely.

TAIL:
Using 4mm (UK 8; US 6) needles, cast on 6 sts in yarn A.
Row 1 (WS): purl.
Row 2: kfb, k4, kfb (8 sts).
Row 3: purl.
Row 4: kfb, k6, kfb (10 sts).
Row 5: purl.
Row 6: kfb, k8, kfb (12 sts).
Row 7: purl.
Row 8: kfb, k10, kfb (14 sts).
Row 9: purl.
Row 10: kfb, k12, kfb (16 sts).
Row 11: purl.
Row 12: kfb, k14, kfb (18 sts).
Row 13: purl. Place a stitch marker here.
Change to yarn B.
Rows 14-19: St st.
Change to yarn A.
Rows 20-25: St st.
Change to yarn B.
Rows 26-30: St st.
Change to yarn A.
Rows 31-35: St st starting with a p row.
Change to yarn B.
Rows 36-40: St st.
Change to yarn A.
Rows 41-45: St st starting with a p row.

Change to yarn B.
Row 46: (k1, k2tog) six times (12 sts).
Row 47: purl.
Row 48: (k2tog) six times (6 sts).
Break yarn and thread through rem sts, pull tight and fasten off securely.

MUZZLE:
Using 4mm needles (UK 8; US 6) needles, cast on 16 sts in yarn A.
Rows 1 (WS)-3: St st starting with a p row.
Row 4: (k2, k2tog) four times (12 sts).
Rows 5-7: St st starting with a p row.
Row 8: (k2tog) six times (6 sts).
Row 9: purl.
Break yarn and thread through rem sts, pull tight and fasten off securely.

EAR (make two):
Using 4mm (UK 8; US 6) needles, cast on 8 sts in yarn A.
Row 1 (WS): purl.
Row 2: k2tog, k4, k2tog (6 sts).
Row 3: purl.
Row 4: k2tog, k2, k2tog (4 sts).
Row 5: purl.
Row 6: (k2tog) twice (2 sts).
Break yarn and thread through rem sts, pull tight and fasten off securely.

FRONT LEG (make two):
Using 4mm (UK 8; US 6) needles, cast on 4 sts in yarn A.
Row 1 (WS): purl.
Row 2: kfb, k2, kfb (6 sts).
Row 3: purl.
Row 4: kfb, k4, kfb (8 sts).
Row 5: purl.
Row 6: kfb, k6, kfb (10 sts).
Rows 7-11: St st starting with a p row.
Row 12: cast on 3 sts, k to end (13 sts). Place a stitch marker here.
Row 13: cast on 3 sts, p to end (16 sts).
Rows 14 and 15: St st.
Row 16: (k2, k2tog) four times (12 sts).
Rows 17-23: St st starting with a p row.
Cast/bind off.

REAR LEG (make two):
Using 4mm (UK 8; US 6) needles, cast on 6 sts in yarn A.
Row 1 (RS): (kfb) six times (12 sts).
Row 2: purl.
Row 3: (k1, kfb) six times (18 sts).

Rows 4–8: St st starting with a p row.
Row 9: cast on 6 sts, k to end (24 sts). Place a stitch marker here.
Row 10: cast on 6 sts, p to end (30 sts).
Rows 11 and 12: St st.
Row 13: (k3, k2tog) six times (24 sts).

Row 14: purl.
Row 15: (k2, k2tog) six times (18 sts).
Row 16: purl.
Row 17: (k1, k2tog) six times (12 sts).
Row 18–20: St st.
Cast/bind off.

STAGE 2: SEWING UP

1. With right sides facing, sew together the row ends of the body with yarn A, leaving a 4–5cm (1½–2in) gap in the middle for stuffing into later.

2. With right sides facing, sew together the row ends of the head with yarn A, leaving the cast-on edge open and creating a round cup shape.

3. The muzzle is slightly pointed in shape. With right sides facing, sew together the row ends with yarn A, leaving the cast-on edge open.

4. With right sides facing and using yarn A, sew together the row ends of the front legs between Rows 12 (marker) and 23, leaving the cast-on edges and the top of the legs open.

5. With right sides facing and using yarn A, sew together the row ends of the rear legs between Rows 9 (marker) and 20, leaving the cast-on edges and the top of the legs open.

6. With right sides facing, sew up the tail between Rows 13 (marker) and 48.

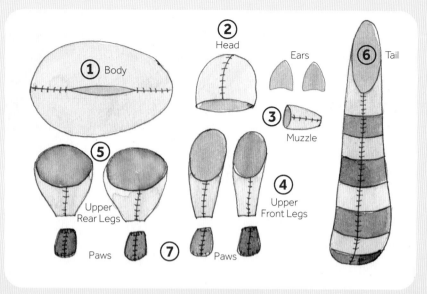

7. With wrong sides facing, sew together the row ends of the paws with yarn A, placing the seam centrally to the underside of each paw. Overstitch/whipstitch the wider toe end to draw in the centres of each paw and create indents.

8. Fasten in all loose ends before wet felting, as these can get in the way. Turn the hollow pieces the right way out.

STAGE 3: WET FELTING

1. Wet felt the body and tail for Rocky, following the wet felting information on page 30.

2. Wet felt the remaining pieces, following the information on page 31.

3. When all the pieces are felted equally, rinse them off. Pull the ears into shape; the remaining hollow pieces can be stuffed with kitchen roll.

4. Leave all the pieces to dry completely.

STAGE 4: STUFFING & CONSTRUCTION

1. Stuff the body firmly and sew up the gap with yarn A.

2. Stuff the head and pin it into position, referring to the diagram below. When you are happy with your positioning, sew the head in place with yarn A using small, close stitches. Add extra stuffing before completely closing up, if required.

3. Stuff the muzzle and pin it to the front of the head, as shown in the diagram below. Sew it into position with yarn A.

4. Pin then sew the paws onto the bottoms of the front and rear legs with yarn A.

5. Stuff the front and rear legs and pin them into position on the body, as shown in the diagram below. Take some time pinning the limbs, to ensure Rocky stands steadily on a flat surface. Once you are happy with the leg positioning, sew them in place with yarn A. Add extra stuffing into the tops of the legs before completely closing them up, if necessary.

6. Position and pin the ears onto the top of the head. Sew the bases in place with yarn A.

7. Stuff the tail and pin it into position at the back of the body. Remember that it curls round to one side of the body, so take some time to reposition the tail, if necessary, to make sure it sits nicely. When you are happy with the positioning, sew the tail in place using yarn A.

STAGE 5: NEEDLE FELTING & DETAILS

1. Raccoons have a fluffy appearance, so a layer of natural grey roving makes a nice finish. I used grey wool roving for this. Add a base layer of fur all over the body, back of the head and legs, following the instructions for flat fur on page 39.

2. Following the Shorty, Tufty Fur instructions on page 42, alternate between lengths of grey roving and black merino wool tops to add corresponding stripy fur along the tail. To encourage the fibres to run in one direction, run the end of the felting needle through the fibres, like combing the fur. Once you are happy, trim the fur on the tail as desired.

3. Follow the flat fur instructions once again to cover the muzzle with natural white fleece, needle felting until it lies flat. To add the white, tufty stripe detail above the eyes, lay a small, narrow length of natural white fleece across the face. Needle felt it in place, working from the centre outwards; leave the ends loose for effect. Trim the ends so that they are approximately 2cm (¾in) long at each side of the face.

4. Using the same technique, add black merino wool tops stripes over each eye area, using the photo detail as a guide (see page 87).

5. Using the steel-grey merino wool tops and following the Nose technique on page 50, add the vertical stripe to Rocky's face: lay a strip vertically up the centre of the nose and face, from the tip of the muzzle to the forehead, then needle felt in place.

6. Make detailed eyes for Rocky, using the instructions on page 51 as a guide: the order of merino wool tops colours, from base to top, is steel-grey, black then white.

7. Follow the instructions on page 54 to add the inner ear colour for Rocky, using the steel-grey merino wool tops.

8. Follow the instructions on page 53 to make the shaped nose for Rocky, using black merino wool tops.

9. 'Draw' the lines of the mouth with twisted black merino wool tops, following the Linear Details technique on page 54.

PEBBLE THE SEAL & PIP THE SEAL PUP

This mother and baby seal are inseparable. They are both knitted using aran (worsted) weight yarn, and only easy needle-felting techniques are used to finish them off – making this family a breeze to make. You could try adding some dotted markings to Pebble, too, to personalize her.

Difficulty

• Easy

What you need

• Yarn

▷ 80g (3oz) of Woolyknit Aran in Pirate Grey, or equivalent aran (worsted) weight 100% pure wool yarn in dark grey, for Pebble; 50g/85yd/77m [A]

▷ 30g (1oz) of Woolyknit Aran in Cream, or equivalent aran (worsted) weight 100% pure wool yarn in cream, for Pip; 50g/85yd/77m [B]

• Felting fibres

▷ Black, white and light-grey merino wool tops
▷ Charcoal grey wool roving
▷ Natural white fleece

• Toy filling

• Nylon fishing wire, for the whiskers

Needles

• One pair of 5mm (UK 6; US 8) needles
• Tapestry needle
• Set of three needle-felting needles in sizes 40, 38 and 32

Tension/gauge

• 18 sts x 24 rows in a 10cm (4in) square over St st, using 5mm (UK 6; US 8) needles

INSTRUCTIONS

STAGE 1: THE KNIT BIT

Pebble the Seal

BODY:
Using 5mm (UK 6; US 8) needles, cast on 2 sts in yarn A.
Row 1 (WS): purl.
Row 2: (kfb) twice (4 sts).
Row 3: purl.
Row 4: kfb, k2, kfb (6 sts).
Row 5: purl.
Row 6: kfb, k4, kfb (8 sts).
Row 7: purl.
Row 8: (kfb) eight times (16 sts).
Row 9: purl.
Row 10: (k1, kfb) eight times (24 sts).
Row 11: purl.
Row 12: (k2, kfb) eight times (32 sts).
Row 13: purl.
Row 14: (k3, kfb) eight times (40 sts).
Row 15: purl.
Row 16: (k4, kfb) eight times (48 sts).
Rows 17–33: St st starting with a p row.
Row 34: (k4, k2tog) eight times (40 sts).
Rows 35–41: St st starting with a p row.
Row 42: (k3, k2tog) eight times (32 sts).
Rows 43–51: St st starting with a p row.
Row 52: (k2, k2tog) eight times (24 sts).
Rows 53–59: St st starting with a p row.
Row 60: (k1, k2tog) eight times (16 sts).
Rows 61–63: St st starting with a p row.
Row 64: (k2tog) eight times (8 sts).
Break yarn and thread through rem sts, pull tight and fasten off securely.

HEAD:
Using 5mm (UK 6; US 8) needles, cast on 6 sts in yarn A.
Row 1 (RS): (kfb) six times (12 sts).
Row 2: purl.
Row 3: (k1, kfb) six times (18 sts).
Row 4: purl.
Row 5: (k2, kfb) six times (24 sts).
Rows 6–8: St st.
Row 9: (k3, kfb) six times (30 sts).
Rows 10–12: St st.
Row 13: (k4, kfb) six times (36 sts).
Rows 14–18: St st.

Row 19: (k4, k2tog) six times (30 sts).
Row 20: purl.
Row 21: (k3, k2tog) six times (24 sts).
Row 22: purl.
Row 23: (k2, k2tog) six times (18 sts).
Row 24: purl.
Row 25: (k1, k2tog) six times (12 sts).
Row 26: purl.
Row 27: (k2tog) six times (6 sts).
Break yarn and thread through rem sts, pull tight and fasten off securely.

FRONT FLIPPER (make two):
Using 5mm (UK 6; US 8) needles, cast on 6 sts in yarn A.
Rows 1 (WS)–3: St st starting with a p row.
Row 4: kfb, k4, kfb (8 sts).
Rows 5–21: St st starting with a p row.
Row 22: k2tog, k4, k2tog (6 sts).
Row 23: purl.
Row 24: k2tog, k2, k2tog (4 sts).
Row 25: purl.
Row 26: kfb, k2, kfb (6 sts).
Row 27: purl.
Row 28: kfb, k4, kfb (8 sts).
Rows 29–41: St st starting with a p row.
Break yarn and thread through rem sts, pull tight and fasten off securely.

BACK FLIPPER (make two):
Using 5mm (UK 6; US 8) needles, cast on 4 sts in yarn A.
Row 1 (WS): purl.
Row 2: kfb, k2, kfb (6 sts).
Rows 3–7: St st starting with a p row.
Row 8: kfb, k4, kfb (8 sts).
Rows 9–11: St st starting with a p row.
Row 12: k2tog, k4, k2tog (6 sts).
Row 13: purl.
Row 14: k2tog, k2, k2tog (4 sts).
Row 15: purl.
Row 16: (k2tog) twice (2 sts).
Row 17: purl.
Row 18: (kfb) twice (4 sts).
Row 19: purl.
Row 20: kfb, k2, kfb (6 sts).
Row 21: purl.
Row 22: kfb, k4, kfb (8 sts).
Rows 23–25: St st starting with a p row.
Row 26: k2tog, k4, k2tog (6 sts).
Rows 27–31: St st starting with a p row.
Row 32: k2tog, k2, k2tog (4 sts).
Cast/bind off purlwise.

Pip the Seal Pup

BODY:

Using 5mm (UK 6; US 8) needles, cast on 6 sts in yarn B.
Row 1 (WS): purl.
Row 2: (kfb) six times (12 sts).
Row 3: purl.
Row 4: (k1, kfb) six times (18 sts).
Row 5: purl.
Row 6: (k2, kfb) six times (24 sts).
Row 7: purl.
Row 8: (k3, kfb) six times (30 sts).
Rows 9-17: St st starting with a p row.
Row 18: (k3, k2tog) six times (24 sts).
Rows 19-21: St st starting with a p row.
Row 22: (k2, k2tog) six times (18 sts).
Rows 23-27: St st starting with a p row.
Row 28: (k1, k2tog) six times (12 sts).
Rows 29-31: St st starting with a p row.
Row 32: (k2tog) six times (6 sts).
Row 33: purl.
Break yarn and thread through rem sts, pull tight and fasten off securely.

HEAD:

Using 5mm (UK 6; US 8) needles, cast on 6 sts in yarn B.
Row 1 (WS): purl.
Row 2: (kfb) six times (12 sts).
Row 3: purl.
Row 4: (k1, kfb) six times (18 sts).
Row 5: purl.
Row 6: (k2, kfb) six times (24 sts).
Rows 7-11: St st starting with a p row.
Row 12: k2tog, k20, k2tog (22 sts).
Row 13: purl.
Cast/bind off.

MUZZLE:

Using 5mm (UK 6; US 8) needles, cast on 14 sts in yarn B.
Rows 1 (WS)-3: St st starting with a p row.
Row 4: k2tog seven times (7 sts).
Break yarn and thread through rem sts, pull tight and fasten off securely.

FRONT FLIPPER (make two):

Using 5mm (UK 6; US 8) needles, cast on 3 sts in yarn B.
Row 1 (RS): (kfb) three times (6 sts).
Row 2: purl.
Row 3: (k1, kfb) three times (9 sts).
Row 4: purl.
Row 5: kfb, k7, kfb (11 sts).
Rows 6-8: St st.
Cast/bind off.

BACK FLIPPER (make two):

Using 5mm (UK 6; US 8) needles, cast on 10 sts in yarn B.
Rows 1 (WS)-5: St st starting with a p row.
Row 6: k2tog, k6, k2tog (8 sts).
Row 7: p2tog, p4, p2tog (6 sts).
Row 8: k2tog, k2, k2tog (4 sts).
Break yarn and thread through rem sts, pull tight and fasten off securely.

Seal flippers

One finished back flipper.

1. These are shaped a bit like a moustache!

2. Bring the two sections wrong sides together and pin them in place. Thread one of the tails of yarn onto your tapestry needle. Take the needle through the top row of edge stitches, across the gap, to bring them together. Pull firmly. Then take the needle below this first stitch across your edge stitches from the opposite side. Pull firmly to secure the second stitch.

3. Repeat this process all the way around to sew up one flipper piece fully. Once you have finished sewing up the flipper, follow the instructions on page 28 to sew in and cut the loose tails of yarn. Make the second flipper in the same way.

STAGE 2: SEWING UP

Pebble the Seal

1. With right sides facing, sew together the row ends of the body with yarn A, leaving a space open where the head is to be attached.

2. With right sides facing, sew together the row ends of the head with yarn A; sew only part way from each end, leaving a space the same size as the space in the body.

3. Sew the head to the body around the opening, leaving a V-shaped opening under the chin for stuffing into later.

4. Using the seal flipper instructions above as a guide, fold each front flipper piece wrong sides together along the narrowest point (there is one longer side, this is correct). Sew the edges together with yarn B.

5. Using the seal flipper instructions above as a guide, fold each back flipper piece wrong sides together at the narrowest point. Sew the edges together with yarn B.

6. Fasten in all loose ends before wet felting, as these can get in the way. Turn all hollow pieces the right way out.

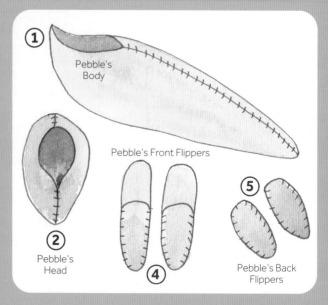

① Pebble's Body

Pebble's Front Flippers

② Pebble's Head

④

⑤ Pebble's Back Flippers

STAGE 2: SEWING UP

Pip the Seal Pup

1. With right sides facing, sew together the row ends of the body with yarn B, leaving a 4–5cm (1½–2in) gap in the middle for stuffing into later.

2. With right sides facing, sew together the row ends of the head with yarn B, leaving the cast-on edge open and creating a round cup shape.

3. With right sides facing, sew together the row ends of the muzzle with yarn B, leaving the cast-on edge open and creating a small round cup shape.

4. Using the seal flipper instructions opposite as a guide, fold each front and back flipper piece wrong sides together, along the narrowest point. Sew the edges together with yarn B.

5. Fasten in all loose ends before wet felting, as these can get in the way. Turn all hollow pieces the right way out.

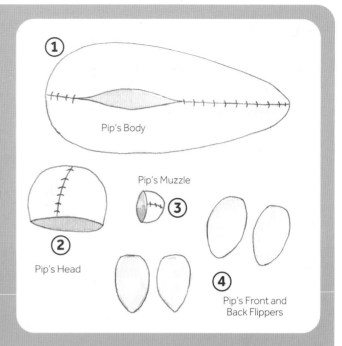

① Pip's Body

② Pip's Head

Pip's Muzzle ③

④ Pip's Front and Back Flippers

STAGE 3: WET FELTING

1. Wet felt the bodies for Pebble and Pip, and the head for Pebble, following the wet felting information on page 30.

2. Wet felt the flippers for Pebble and Pip, and Pip's head and muzzle, following the wet felting information on page 31.

3. When all the pieces are felted equally, rinse them off. Pull the flippers into shape; the remaining hollow pieces can be stuffed with kitchen roll.

4. Leave all the pieces to dry completely.

STAGE 4: STUFFING & CONSTRUCTION

Pebble the Seal

1. Start off with the body and head. Stuff both firmly and sew up the gap under the chin with yarn A.

2. Position, pin and then sew the front flippers to the body with yarn A – the thinner, single layered part of the flipper lays flat against the body, with the double-layered part of the flipper coming away from the body.

3. Position, pin and then attach the back flippers to the body with yarn A – these are sewn to the tail end of the body, then sewn to each other at the base and side edges on the inside, as seen in the photo detail bottom left.

4. Sew a running stitch around the muzzle of the face with yarn A and gently pull to gather the end of the head a little, creating the shaping for a nose. Secure this with a few tiny anchor stitches, then take the needle through the back of the head and cut the yarn flush to hide the end.

Pip the Seal Pup

1. Stuff the body firmly and sew up the gap underneath with yarn B using small, close stitches.

2. Stuff and pin the head into position as shown on the diagram. Sew the head in place with yarn B using small, close stitches. Add extra stuffing before completely closing up, if required.

3. Stuff and pin the muzzle into position as shown on the diagram. Sew the muzzle in place with yarn B using small, close stitches. Add extra stuffing before completely closing up, if required.

4. Pin the front flippers onto the body, as shown on the diagram. Sew in place with yarn B using small, close stitches.

5. Pin the back flippers onto the body, as shown on the diagram. Sew in place with yarn B, in the same way as the back flippers for Pebble, left, in step 4.

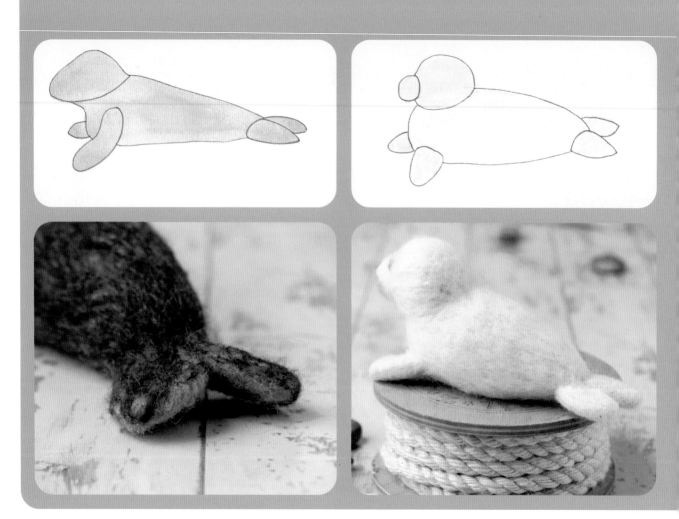

STAGE 5: NEEDLE FELTING & DETAILS

Pebble the Seal

1. Following the instructions on page 39, attach a base layer of flat fur all over Pebble's body and flippers, excluding the tummy, using charcoal grey wool roving. This will hide the seams and blend the shape of the muzzle on the head. When adding the roving to the flippers, use a foam block or rice bag to protect your fingers and to provide a surface to work against.

2. For extra realism, needle felt an oval-shaped layer of natural white fleece to the underside of Pebble, from the rear fins up to the bottom of the neck area, until it lies flat. To 'knock back' the colour a little, needle felt a wispy layer of charcoal grey wool roving over the top. If you wish, dot wispy layers of natural white fleece across Pebble's body as I have done and, again, knock them back with thin layers of charcoal grey wool roving.

3. Lay a circle of light grey merino wool tops over the nose and mouth area of Pebble's face then needle felt it in place.

4. Roll two tiny balls with the black merino wool tops and needle felt them to the end of the muzzle to add nostrils – apply the stretching technique described in step 2 of the Detailed Eyes technique on page 51, to shape them into slight ovals with your needle.

5. 'Draw' the lines of the mouth with twisted black merino wool tops, following the Linear Details instructions on page 54.

6. Make detailed eyes for Pebble, using the instructions on page 51 as a guide: the order of merino wool tops colours, from base to top, is light grey, black then white.

7. Add Pebble's whiskers following the instructions on page 57.

Pip the Seal Pup

1. Following the instructions on page 39, attach a base layer of flat fur all over Pip's body, head and flippers, using natural white fleece. This will hide the seams and blend the shape of the muzzle on the head. When adding the fleece to the flippers, use a foam block or rice bag to protect your fingers and to provide a surface to work against.

2. To add the distinctive fluffy fur of a baby seal, follow the Fluffy Fur instructions on page 41.

3. Make detailed eyes for Pip using the instructions on page 51 as a guide: the order of merino wool tops colours, from base to top, is black then white.

4. To define Pip's eyes a little more, add eyelids above and below using the white merino wool tops. These are made and added in a similar way to the eyebrows on page 52: roll a tiny, thin sausage shape and circle it around one eye. Needle felt it in place. Repeat with the other eye.

5. With the black merino wool tops, roll a small ball then needle felt it to the end of the muzzle to make a nose – apply the stretching technique described in step 2 of the Detailed Eyes technique on page 51, to shape it into a slight oval with your needle.

6. 'Draw' the lines of the mouth with twisted black merino wool tops, following the Linear Details instructions on page 54.

7. As Pip is a young seal, his whiskers haven't grown in yet! However, if you wish to add them, follow the instructions on page 57.

SAVANNA THE LION

Savanna sits in his grassland, majestic and relaxed. He is a sight to behold with his beautiful mane and proud face. There is a little bit of complex detailing around the face to needle felt, but when it comes to adding the fur I have deliberately chosen a yarn that felts with a fuzzy texture, which means less needle felting later on! Furthermore, Savanna is made with aran (worsted) weight yarn, making this larger project still relatively quick to knit.

Difficulty

• Intermediate to Difficult

What you need

• Yarn

▷ *150g (5¼oz) of Lopi Lettlopi in Barley, or equivalent aran (worsted) weight 100% pure wool yarn in variegated warm-yellow brown; 50g/110yd/100m [A]*

▷ *Small amount of dark-brown yarn, for the paws*

• Felting fibres

▷ *White, gold, pink and black merino wool tops*

▷ *Warm yellow-brown, light-brown sandy yellow, gold yellow and light grey wool roving OR ready-blended gold-yellow wool roving, for the hair*

▷ *Warm yellow-brown and dark brown wool roving, for the tail*

▷ *Natural white fleece*

• Toy filling

• Stitch marker (a contrasting-coloured scrap of yarn makes a handy, economical alternative)

Needles

• One pair of 5mm (UK 6; US 8) needles

• Tapestry needle

• Set of three needle-felting needles in sizes 40, 38 and 32

Tension/gauge

• 18 sts x 24 rows in a 10cm (4in) square over St st, using 5mm (UK 6; US 8) needles

INSTRUCTIONS

STAGE 1: THE KNIT BIT

BODY:
Using 5mm (UK 6; US 8) needles, cast on 20 sts in yarn A.
Row 1 (WS): purl.
Row 2: (kfb) twenty times (40 sts).
Row 3: purl.
Row 4: (k1, kfb) twenty times (60 sts).
Row 5: purl.
Row 6: (k2, kfb) twenty times (80 sts).
Rows 7-9: St st starting with a p row.
Row 10: (k4, kfb) sixteen times (96 sts).
Rows 11-13: St st starting with a p row.
Row 14: (k6, k2tog) twelve times (84 sts).
Rows 15-17: St st starting with a p row.
Row 18: (k5, k2tog) twelve times (72 sts).
Row 19-33: St st starting with a p row.
Row 34: (k4, k2tog) twelve times (60 sts).
Row 35-53: St st starting with a p row.
Row 54: (k4, kfb) twelve times (72 sts).
Row 55-57: St st starting with a p row.
Row 58: (k5, kfb) twelve times (84 sts).
Row 59-67: St st starting with a p row.
Row 68: (k5, k2tog) twelve times (72 sts).
Row 69: purl.
Row 70: (k4, k2tog) twelve times (60 sts).
Row 71: purl.
Row 72: (k3, k2tog) twelve times (48 sts).
Row 73: purl.
Row 74: (k2, k2tog) twelve times (36 sts).
Row 75: purl.
Row 76: (k1, k2tog) twelve times (24 sts).
Row 77: purl.
Row 78: (k2tog) twelve times (12 sts).
Break yarn and thread through rem sts, pull tight and fasten off securely.

HEAD:
Using 5mm (UK 6; US 8) needles, cast on 60 sts in yarn A.
Rows 1 (WS)-3: St st starting with a p row.
Row 4: (k3, k2tog) twelve times (48 sts).
Row 5: purl.
Row 6: (k3, kfb) twelve times (60 sts).
Rows 7-17: St st starting with a p row.
Row 18: (k3, k2tog) twelve times (48 sts).
Rows 19-21: St st starting with a p row.
Row 22: (k2, k2tog) twelve times (36 sts).
Row 23: purl.
Row 24: (k1, k2tog) twelve times (24 sts).
Row 25: purl.
Row 26: (k2tog) twelve times (12 sts).
Row 27: purl.
Row 28: (k2tog) six times (6 sts).
Break yarn and thread through rem sts, pull tight and fasten off securely.

MUZZLE:
Using 5mm (UK 6; US 8) needles, cast on 30 sts in yarn A.
Rows 1 (WS)-3: St st starting with a p row.
Row 4: (k3, k2tog) six times (24 sts).
Rows 5-9: St st starting with a p row.
Row 10: (k2tog) twelve times (12 sts).
Row 11: purl.
Row 12: (k2tog) six times (6 sts).
Break yarn and thread through rem sts, pull tight and fasten off securely.

EAR (make two):
Using 5mm (UK 6; US 8) needles, cast on 16 sts in yarn A.
Rows 1 (WS)-3: St st starting with a p row.
Row 4: k2tog, k12, k2tog (14 sts).
Row 5: purl.
Row 6: k2tog, k10, k2tog (12 sts).
Row 7: purl.
Row 8: k2tog, k8, k2tog (10 sts).
Row 9: purl.
Row 10: k2tog, k6, k2tog (8 sts).
Row 11: purl.
Row 12: k2tog, k4, k2tog (6 sts).
Break yarn and thread through rem sts, pull tight and fasten off securely.

FRONT LEG (make two):
Using 5mm (UK 6; US 8) needles, cast on 4 sts in yarn A.
Row 1 (WS): purl.
Row 2: (kfb) four times (8 sts).
Row 3: purl.
Row 4: (k1, kfb) four times (12 sts).
Row 5: purl.
Row 6: (k2, kfb) four times (16 sts).
Rows 7-11: St st starting with a p row.
Row 12: cast on 8 sts, k to end (24 sts). Place a stitch marker here.
Row 13: cast on 8 sts, p to end. (32 sts).
Rows 14 and 15: St st.
Row 16: k2tog, k28, k2tog (30 sts).
Row 17: purl.
Row 18: k2tog, k26, k2tog (28 sts).
Row 19: purl.
Row 20: (k5, k2tog) four times (24 sts).
Rows 21-25: St st starting with a p row.
Row 26: (k4, k2tog) four times (20 sts).
Rows 27-29: St st starting with a p row.
Row 30: (k3, k2tog) four times (16 sts).
Rows 31-35: St st starting with a p row.
Row 36: k2tog, k12, k2tog (14 sts).
Row 37: purl.
Row 38: kfb, k5, (kfb) twice, k5, kfb (18 sts).
Rows 39-43: St st starting with a p row.
Row 44: (k1, k2tog) six times (12 sts).
Break yarn and thread through rem sts, pull tight and fasten off securely.

REAR LEG:
Using 5mm (UK 6; US 8) needles, cast on 6 sts in yarn A.
Row 1 (WS): purl.
Row 2: (kfb) six times (12 sts).
Row 3: purl.
Row 4: (k1, kfb) six times (18 sts).
Row 5: purl.
Row 6: (k2, kfb) six times (24 sts).
Row 7: purl.
Row 8: (k3, kfb) six times (30 sts).
Rows 9–17: St st starting with a p row.
Row 18: k2tog, k19, *turn*, leave rem 9 sts unworked (20 sts).
Row 19: purl.
Row 20: k2tog, k16, k2tog (18 sts).
Row 21: purl.
Row 22: k2tog, k14, k2tog (16 sts).
Row 23: purl.
Row 24: k2tog, k12, k2tog (14 sts).
Row 25: purl.
Row 26: (k2tog) seven times (7 sts).
Row 27: purl.
Break yarn and thread through rem sts, pull tight and fasten off securely.

Note: *this next section is working from the hip towards the paw, using the unworked stitches on Row 18.*
Row 1 (RS): working the 9 rem sts from Row 18, k9 sts (18 sts).
Rows 2–14: St st.
Row 15: (k2, k2tog) twice, k2, (k2, k2tog) twice (14 sts).
Row 16: purl.
Row 17: (k2tog) seven times (7 sts).
Break yarn and thread through rem sts, pull tight and fasten off securely.

REAR PAW:
Using 5mm (UK 6; US 8) needles, cast on 18 sts in yarn A.
Rows 1 (WS)–11: St st starting with a p row.
Row 12: (k2, k2tog) twice, k2, (k2, k2tog) twice (14 sts).
Row 13: purl.
Row 14: (k2tog) seven times (7 sts).
Break yarn and thread through rem sts, pull tight and fasten off securely.

TAIL:
Using 5mm (UK 6; US 8) needles, cast on 16 sts in yarn A.
Rows 1 (WS)–25: St st starting with a p row.
Row 26: k2tog, k12, k2tog (14 sts).
Rows 27–41: St st starting with a p row.
Row 42: k2tog, k10, k2tog (12 sts).
Rows 43–51: St st starting with a p row.
Row 52: k2tog, k8, k2tog (10 sts).
Rows 53–61: St st starting with a p row.
Row 62: k2tog, k6, k2tog (8 sts).
Rows 63–67: St st starting with a p row.
Row 68: (k2tog) four times (4 sts).
Break yarn and thread through rem sts, pull tight and fasten off securely.

- TURNING YOUR KNITTING -

When you 'turn' your knitting, you are literally turning it part way through the row you are working on, before you have 'finished' the row. To continue you begin a new row, working only on the stitches you have knitted before the turn. This creates shape, and is something sock knitters use all the time.

STAGE 2: SEWING UP

1. Using the remaining tail from the cast on, sew a running stitch through the 20 cast-on stitches then pull the tail to bring them together. Secure in place, following the instructions on page 28.

2. With right sides facing, sew together the row ends of the body with yarn A, leaving a 5–6cm (2–2½in) gap in the middle for stuffing into later.

3. With right sides facing, sew together the row ends of the head with yarn A, leaving the cast-on edge open to create a large cup shape.

4. With right sides facing, sew together the row ends of the muzzle with yarn A, leaving the cast-on edge open to create a smaller cup shape.

5. With right sides facing, sew together the row ends of the front legs between Rows 12 (marker) and 45, using yarn A.

6. With right sides facing, fold over the smaller 'foot' section of the sitting rear leg to form an open cup shape. Following the diagram above right for the shape and indication of where to sew, use yarn A to sew together the row ends of the foot.

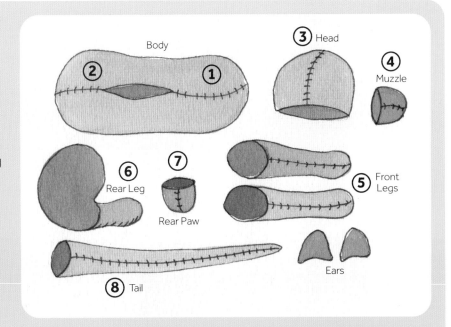

7. With right sides facing, sew together the row ends of the rear paw with yarn A to form an open cup shape.

8. With right sides facing, sew together the row ends of the tail with yarn A, leaving the cast-on edge open.

9. Fasten in all loose ends as these can get in the way when felting. Turn all hollow pieces the right way out before wet felting.

STAGE 3: WET FELTING

1. Wet felt the body and head pieces for Savanna, following the information on page 30.

2. Wet felt the remaining body parts, following the information on page 31.

3. When all the pieces are wet felted, rinse them off. Pull the ears and leg of the rear leg into shape; the remaining hollow pieces (and the foot of the rear leg) can be stuffed with kitchen roll.

4. Leave all the pieces to dry completely.

STAGE 4: STUFFING & CONSTRUCTION

1. Stuff the body firmly then sew up the gap with yarn A.

2. Stuff the head and pin it into position on the body, referring to the diagram. When you are happy with your positioning, sew the head in place with yarn A using small, close stitches. Add extra stuffing before completely closing up, if required.

3. Stuff the muzzle then pin it into position on the head, the seam facing down, using the diagram below to help you. I have chosen to make my lion face towards the left, but you may wish to make him face in another direction. Sew the muzzle in place with yarn A, using small, close stitches.

4. Stuff the front legs then pin them into position on the body, as shown in the diagram. Sew them to the body with yarn A, using small, close stitches. Add extra stuffing in the 'shoulders' before sewing up the legs completely, if required.

5. Stuff the foot of the rear leg then pin the leg into position on the body, as shown in the diagram. Take some time pinning it, to ensure that Savanna sits steadily on a flat surface. Once you are happy with your positioning, sew the rear leg in place with yarn A. Add extra stuffing in the 'hip' before sewing up the leg completely.

6. Stuff, position and pin the rear paw onto the body, as shown in the diagram. Sew it in place with yarn A, using small, close stitches.

7. Position and pin the ears as shown in the diagram below. Sew the base of the ears in place with yarn A.

8. Stuff the tail then pin it into position at the rear end of the body. Sew the tail in place with yarn A, using small, close stitches. Note: the diagram below shows the tail curled towards the paws, achieved by stitching the end of the tail to the centre of the body using tiny anchor stitches – do not do this yet, as this can make needle felting more difficult.

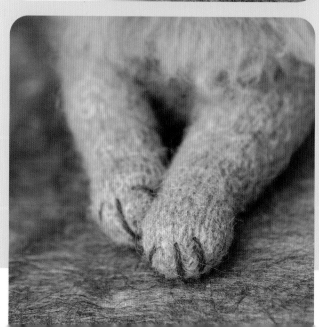

STAGE 5: NEEDLE FELTING & DETAILS

NOTE: I liked the texture and colour of my lion, so have not added a needle-felted base layer of fibres to the main body, paws, ears or tail.

1. Begin with the head. Following the instructions on page 39, lay a thin base layer of flat fur all over the face area using the warm yellow-brown roving.

2. Create eye sockets for your lion, following the instructions on page 48.

3. You may need to build up the nose with several lengths of roving to create the strong, smooth and recognizable profile of a lion's face. Following the instructions on page 50, use a few folded lengths of warm-yellow brown roving to sculpt Savanna's nose.

4. Make the detailed eyes for Savanna, using the instructions on page 51 as a guide: the order of merino wool tops colours, from base to top, is white, black, gold then white.

5. Following the instructions in steps 1 and 2 on page 52, create eyebrow shapes to form the strong brow line and bridge of the nose for Savanna. Cover the top edge of the golden part of the eye slightly, for a more natural look.

6. Twist two thin lengths of black merino wool tops and needle felt each one at the base of each brow, right at the top of the eyes, to form an eyelash line. This gives further definition to the eyes of the lion.

7. 'Draw' the lines of the mouth with twisted black merino wool tops, following the Linear Details instructions on page 54.

8. The nose of the lion is made with two colours. To start, pull a small amount from the black merino wool tops. Fold them into an inverted (upside down) triangular shape and place the shape at the end of the nose. Whilst needling it into position you can pull down the bottom point with the needle to make it slimmer and long enough to join the mouth line detail. Repeat this process to create the smaller triangular nose detail with the pink merino wool tops, as shown in the top photograph on the opposite page.

9. The bottom of the lion's chin is white. Fill the triangular space with a small amount of natural white fleece, following the Cheeks/Mouths instructions on page 49. If necessary, fluff it up slightly with a few flicks of the needle, as described in the Fluffy Fur instructions on page 41. Then, add very thin, flat layers of natural fleece to the left and right of the nose and mouth, following the instructions for base flat fur on page 39. Roll and needle felt several tiny black balls of black merino wool tops and dot these in twos or threes onto each 'cheek' to indicate whisker pores.

10. The most distinctive part of a lion is his luscious mane! In order to make this as natural as possible I recommend blending a few colours together, in the same way described on pages 46 and 47. However, ready-blended colours are available to buy, and I have used a mix myself that incorporates sandy, golden and grey tones. To make the mane of the lion, follow the instructions for Long Fur on page 43: start from the base of the head at the back, working around to under the chin, then steadily make your way up to the crown of the head.

11. Once you are happy with the overall layering of the mane, you can give your lion a haircut! Thin out excess fibres with the tip of your felting needle, and trim to length, using steps 6 and 7 on page 47 as a guide. Ensure each 'layer' of long hair that makes up the mane is of even length – for example, if the first bottom layer is 6cm (2¼in) long, the second layer above it should also be the same length.

12. Once the longer section of the mane is in place, add a shorter mane at the very top of the head and in front of the ears, following the Short, Tufty Fur instructions on page 42. This creates a natural ring of hair around the face.

13. To finish the mane of your lion, add a little fibre inside each ear, again following the Short, Tufty Fur instructions on page 42. Remember to use a foam block or rice bag as you work this area, to protect your fingers and to provide a surface to work against.

14. Encourage the fibres of the hair to run in one direction by running the end of the felting needle through the fibres – it is a little like combing hair.

15. Following the instructions on page 55, add the tuft at the end of the tail with dark-brown roving.

16. Sew the toes onto the paws of your lion, following the instructions on page 56.

17. To have your lion's legs in a relaxed position, stitch one front paw at a slight angle to the inside edge of the other paw.

18. Complete your lion by stitching a tiny section of the end of the tail to the hip of the lion, using a tapestry needle and yarn A.

TRUFFLE THE PIG & JELLYBEAN THE PIGLET

Truffle is a proud mum to her daughter, Jellybean. These are pretty in pink and totally adorable as a little family. Knitted using double-knit (light worsted) weight yarn, they also have dainty trotters and simple, fine features.

Difficulty

• Easy

What you need

• Yarn

▷ *75g (2½oz) of Drops Puna in Powder Pink, or equivalent DK (light worsted) weight 100% pure alpaca yarn in pale pink; 50g/120yd/110m [A]*

• Felting fibres

▷ *Black, dark grey, white, pink merino wool tops*
▷ ***Optional:*** *Brown merino wool tops, for Jellybean's spots*

• Toy filling

Needles

• One pair of 4mm (UK 8; US 6) needles
• Tapestry needle
• Set of three needle-felting needles in sizes 40, 38 and 32

Tension/gauge

• 21 sts x 28 rows in a 10cm (4in) square over St st, using 4mm (UK 8; US 6) needles

INSTRUCTIONS

STAGE 1: THE KNIT BIT

Truffle the Pig

BODY & HEAD:
Using 4mm (UK 8; US 6) needles, cast on 50 sts in yarn A.
Row 1 (WS): purl.
Row 2: kfb, k48, kfb (52 sts).
Row 3: purl.
Row 4: kfb, k50, kfb (54 sts).
Row 5: purl.
Row 6: kfb, k52, kfb (56 sts).
Rows 7-9: St st starting with a p row.
Row 10: k2tog, k52, k2tog (54 sts).
Row 11: purl.
Row 12: k2tog, k50, k2tog (52 sts).
Row 13: purl.
Row 14: k2tog, k48, k2tog (50 sts).
Row 15: purl.
Row 16: cast off 5 sts, k to end (45 sts).
Row 17: cast off 5 sts, p to end (40 sts).
Rows 18-35: St st.
Row 36: cast on 5 sts, k to end (45 sts).
Row 37: cast on 5 sts, p to end (50 sts).
Row 38: kfb, k48, kfb (52 sts).
Row 39: purl.
Row 40: kfb, k50, kfb (54 sts).
Row 41: purl.
Row 42: kfb, k52, kfb (56 sts).
Rows 43-45: St st starting with a p row.
Row 46: k2tog, k52, k2tog (54 sts).
Row 47: purl.
Row 48: k2tog, k50, k2tog (52 sts).
Row 49: purl.
Row 50: k2tog, k48, k2tog (50 sts).
Row 51: purl.
Row 52: cast off 5 sts, k to end (45 sts).
Row 53: cast off 5 sts, p to end (40 sts).
Row 54: cast on 3 sts, k to end (43 sts).
Row 55: cast on 3 sts, p to end (46 sts).
Row 56: k2tog, k42, k2tog (44 sts).
Row 57: purl.
Row 58: k2tog, k40, k2tog (42 sts).
Row 59: purl.
Row 60: k2tog, k38, k2tog, (40 sts).
Row 61: purl.
Row 62: (k3, k2tog) eight times (32 sts).
Row 63: purl.

Row 64: (k2, k2tog) eight times (24 sts).
Row 65: purl.
Row 66: (k1, k2tog) eight times (16 sts).
Row 67: purl.
Row 68: k2tog, k12, k2tog (14 sts).
Row 69: purl.
Cast/bind off.

SNOUT END:
Using 4mm (UK 8; US 6) needles, cast on 2 sts in yarn A.
Row 1 (WS): purl.
Row 2: (kfb) twice (4 sts).
Rows 3-5: St st starting with a p row.
Row 6: (k2tog) twice (2 sts).
Break yarn and thread through rem sts, pull tight and fasten off securely.

EAR (make two):
Using 4mm (UK 8; US 6) needles, cast on 8 sts in yarn A.
Row 1 (WS): purl.
Row 2: kfb, k6, kfb (10 sts).
Rows 3-9: St st starting with a p row.
Row 10: k2tog, k6, k2tog (8 sts).
Row 11: purl.
Row 12: k2tog, k4, k2tog (6 sts).
Row 13: purl.
Row 14: k2tog, k2, k2tog (4 sts).
Row 15: purl.
Row 16: (k2tog) twice (2 sts).
Break yarn and thread through rem sts, pull tight and fasten off securely.

TUMMY:
Using 4mm (UK 8; US 6) needles, cast on 4 sts in yarn A.
Row 1 (WS): purl.
Row 2: kfb, k2, kfb (6 sts).
Row 3: purl.
Row 4: kfb, k4, kfb (8 sts).
Row 5: purl.
Row 6: kfb, k6, kfb (10 sts).
Row 7: purl.
Row 8: kfb, k8, kfb (12 sts).

Row 9: purl.
Row 10: kfb, k10, kfb (14 sts).
Row 11: purl.
Row 12: kfb, k12, kfb (16 sts).
Row 13: purl.
Row 14: kfb, k14, kfb (18 sts).
Rows 15-17: St st starting with a p row.
Row 18: k2tog, k14, k2tog (16 sts).
Row 19: purl.
Row 20: k2tog, k12, k2tog (14 sts).
Row 21: purl.
Row 22: k2tog, k10, k2tog (12 sts).
Row 23: purl.
Row 24: k2tog, k8, k2tog (10 sts).
Row 25: purl.
Row 26: k2tog, k6, k2tog (8 sts).
Row 27: purl.
Row 28: k2tog, k4, k2tog (6 sts).
Row 29: purl.
Row 30: k2tog, k2, k2tog (4 sts).
Row 31: purl.
Break yarn and thread through rem sts, pull tight and fasten off securely.

TAIL:
Using 4mm (UK 8; US 6) needles, cast on 26 sts in yarn A.
Rows 1 (WS)-5: St st starting with a p row.
Cast/bind off.

Jellybean the Piglet

BODY & HEAD:
Using 4mm (UK 8; US 6) needles, cast on 6 sts in yarn A.
Row 1 (RS): kfb six times (12 sts).
Row 2: purl.
Row 3: (k1, kfb) six times (18 sts).
Row 4: purl.
Row 5: (k2, kfb) six times (24 sts).
Row 6: purl.
Row 7: (k3, kfb) six times (30 sts).
Rows 8–20: St st.
Row 21: (k3, k2tog) six times (24 sts).
Row 22: purl.
Row 23: k9, (kfb) six times, k9 (30 sts).
Rows 24–26: St st.
Row 27: (k3, k2tog) six times (24 sts).
Row 28: purl.
Row 29: (k2, k2tog) six times (18 sts).
Row 30: purl.
Row 31: (k1, k2tog) six times (12 sts).
Row 32: purl.
Row 33: k2tog, k8, k2tog (10 sts).
Row 34: purl.
Cast/bind off.

SNOUT END:
Using 4mm (UK 8; US 6) needles, cast on 2 sts in yarn A.
Row 1 (RS): (kfb) twice (4 sts).
Row 2: purl.
Row 3: (k2tog) twice (2 sts).
Break yarn and thread through rem sts, pull tight and fasten off securely.

EAR (make two):
Using 4mm (UK 8; US 6) needles, cast on 4 sts in yarn A.
Row 1 (WS): purl.
Row 2: kfb, k2, kfb (6 sts).
Row 3: purl.
Row 4: k2tog, k2, k2tog (4 sts).
Row 5: purl.
Row 6: (k2tog) twice (2 sts).
Break yarn and thread through rem sts, pull tight and fasten off securely.

LEG (make four):
Using 4mm (UK 8; US 6) needles, cast on 10 sts in yarn A.
Row 1 (WS): purl.
Row 2: k2tog, k6, k2tog (8 sts).
Row 3: purl.
Row 4: k2tog, k4, k2tog (6 sts).
Row 5: purl.
Break yarn and thread through rem sts, pull tight and fasten off securely.

TAIL:
Using 4mm (UK 8; US 6) needles, cast on 15 sts in yarn A.
Cast/bind off.

STAGE 2: SEWING UP

Truffle the Pig

1. With right sides facing and referring to the diagram below, sew up the legs on the all-in-one body with yarn A.

2. Pinch the head section of the knitted all-in-one body right sides together, bringing together points A and B, then pin. Sew in place, from the snout to the base of the 'head' with yarn A.

3. Pinch points C and D together then pin. Sew in place, following the instructions on page 23.

4. Still with right sides facing, stitch across the corner at the front and back of the body, at the place indicated by the 'X' on the diagram, using yarn A. Doing this means that, when the body is turned the right way out, there will be a rounded shape at the back for your pig's bottom.

5. Sew the snout end to the bottom of the face, right sides facing, using yarn A.

6. Fasten in all loose ends as these can get in the way when felting. Turn the all-in-one body the right way out.

Jellybean the Piglet

1. With right sides facing, sew together the row ends of the body with yarn A, leaving a 4–5cm (1½–2in) gap in the middle for stuffing into later.

2. Sew the snout end to the bottom of the face, right sides facing, using yarn A.

3. With right sides facing, sew together the row ends of the legs, with yarn A, leaving the cast-on edge open to create pointed cup shapes.

4. Fasten in all loose ends as these can get in the way when felting. Turn all the hollow pieces the right way out.

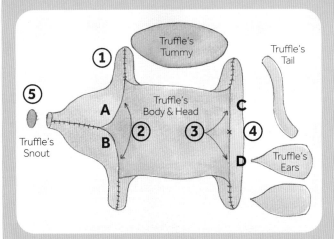

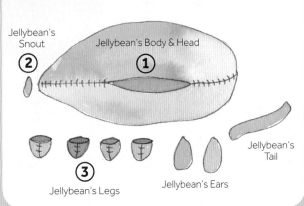

STAGE 3: WET FELTING

Truffle the Pig

1. Wet felt the all-in-one body for Truffle, following the information on page 30.

2. Wet felt the ears and tummy, following the information on page 31.

3. To wet felt the tail, dip it in the hot soapy water and roll the piece between the palms of your hands, so that it becomes a long, rounded shape. This makes it suitable for tying a knot in later.

4. When all the pieces are felted equally, rinse them off. Pull the ears and tummy into shape; the remaining hollow pieces can be stuffed with kitchen roll.

5. Leave all the pieces to dry completely.

Jellybean the Piglet

1. Wet felt the body & head for Jellybean, following the information on page 30.

2. Wet felt the ears and legs following the information on page 31.

3. To wet felt the tail, dip it in the hot soapy water and roll the piece between the palms of your hands, so that it becomes a long, rounded shape. This makes it suitable for tying a knot in later.

4. When all the pieces are felted equally, rinse them off. Pull the ears into shape; the remaining hollow pieces can be stuffed with kitchen roll.

5. Leave all the pieces to dry completely. As the legs are very small, you may need to use a pointed object, like the end of a knitting needle, to open up the cast-on end again after felting.

STAGE 4: STUFFING & CONSTRUCTION

Truffle the Pig

1. Stuff the body and legs firmly, then attach the tummy piece using yarn A. Before closing up the tummy completely, add extra stuffing to make it nice and full.

2. Pin the ears onto the head so that the top points are facing forwards, as shown in the diagram. Sew the base of the ears in place with yarn A.

3. Tie a knot at the end of the tail. Pin the tail into position then sew in place with yarn A.

Jellybean the Piglet

1. Stuff the body & head firmly, making sure that the 'bump' of the head is more pointed and pronounced than the back of the piglet, as shown in the diagram. Sew up the gap underneath with yarn A.

2. Stuff the legs firmly – it's possible to add a little bit of stuffing to the legs by poking it in with the end of a knitting needle. Pin these into position on the body, as shown in the diagram, then sew them in place with yarn A, using small, close stitches.

3. Pin the ears onto the head so that the top points are facing forwards, as shown in the diagram. Sew the base of the ears in place with yarn A.

4. Tie a knot at the end of the tail. Pin the tail into position then sew in place with yarn A.

STAGE 5: NEEDLE FELTING & DETAILS

Truffle the Pig

1. To create a smooth, streamlined look for Truffle, add a thin base layer of flat fur all over the all-in-one body with the pink merino wool tops, following the instructions on page 39. I left the ears uncovered, but you could cover the ears, too, if you wish.

2. Create eye sockets for Truffle, following the instructions for this on page 48.

3. Make detailed eyes for Truffle, using the instructions on page 51 as a guide: the order of merino wool tops colours, from base to top, is black then white.

4. Add two oval-shaped nostrils at the end of the nose with dark-grey merino wool tops, following the Simple Nose instructions on page 53.

5. 'Draw' the lines of the mouth and the trotter details with twisted dark-grey merino wool tops, following the Linear Details instructions on page 54.

Jellybean the Piglet

1. To create a smooth, streamlined look for Jellybean, add a thin base layer of flat fur using the pink merino wool tops, following the instructions on page 39. I left the ears and tail uncovered, but you could cover the ears, too, if you wanted to.

2. Use the dark-grey merino wool tops to make the eyes for Jellybean, following the Simple Eye instructions on page 52.

3. Add two oval-shaped nostrils at the end of the nose with dark-grey merino wool tops, following the Simple Nose instructions on page 53.

4. 'Draw' the lines of the mouth and the trotter details with twisted dark-grey merino wool tops, following the Linear Details instructions on page 54.

- TIP -

Customize your pig and piglets by needle felting flat, oval-shaped spots here and there. Or, research different breeds and use other markings and colours to suit! (See page 45 for inspiration.)

TWIGLET THE KOALA

Twiglet is cuddly and cute by the bucket load! She is definitely a fun project if you want to make an animal that's more unusual. It's amazing how a few simple knitting techniques, combined with some cunning needle-felting tweaks, give her the distinctive koala shape.

Difficulty

- Easy to Intermediate

What you need

- Yarn
  ▷ 120g (4¼oz) of Drops Alaska Grey Mix, or equivalent aran (worsted) weight 100% pure wool yarn in variegated grey; 50g/77yd/70m [A]
  ▷ 20g (¾oz) of Drops Alaska Off White, or equivalent aran (worsted) weight 100% pure wool yarn in cream; 50g/77yd/70m [B]
  ▷ Small amount of dark-grey yarn, for the front and back paws
- Felting fibres
  ▷ Black, dark brown and pink merino wool tops
  ▷ Natural-grey wool roving
  ▷ Natural white fleece, for the tummy and ears
- Toy filling
- Stitch marker (a contrasting-coloured scrap of yarn makes a handy, economical alternative)
- Stitch holder

Needles

- One pair of 5mm (UK 6; US 8) needles
- Tapestry needle
- Set of three needle-felting needles in sizes 40, 38 and 32

Tension/gauge

- 17 sts x 22 rows in a 10cm (4in) square over St st, using 5mm (UK 6; US 8) needles

INSTRUCTIONS

STAGE 1: THE KNIT BIT

BODY:
Using 5mm (UK 6; US 8) needles, cast on 6 sts in yarn A.
Row 1 (WS): purl.
Row 2: (kfb) six times (12 sts).
Row 3: purl.
Row 4: (k1, kfb) six times (18 sts).
Row 5: purl.
Row 6: (k2, kfb) six times (24 sts).
Row 7: purl.
Row 8: (k3, kfb) six times (30 sts).
Row 9: purl.
Row 10: (k4, kfb) six times (36 sts).
Row 11: purl.
Row 12: (k5, kfb) six times (42 sts).
Row 13: purl.
Row 14: (k6, kfb) six times (48 sts).
Row 15: purl.
Row 16: (k7, kfb) six times (54 sts).
Rows 17–31: St st starting with a p row.
Row 32: (k7, k2tog) six times (48 sts).
Row 33: purl.
Row 34: (k6, k2tog) six times (42 sts).
Rows 35–37: St st starting with a p row.
Row 38: (k5, k2tog) six times (36 sts).
Row 39: purl.
Row 40: (k4, k2tog) six times (30 sts).
Row 41: purl.
Row 42: (k3, k2tog) six times (24 sts).
Row 43: purl.
Row 44: (k2, k2tog) six times (18 sts).
Rows 45: purl.
Row 46: (k2tog) nine times (9 sts).
Break yarn and thread through rem sts, pull tight and fasten off securely.

HEAD:
Using 5mm (UK 6; US 8) needles, cast on 8 sts in yarn A.
Row 1 (WS): purl.
Row 2: (kfb) eight times (16 sts).
Row 3: purl.
Row 4: (k1, kfb) eight times (24 sts).
Row 5: purl.
Row 6: (k2, kfb) eight times (32 sts).
Row 7: purl.
Row 8: (k3, kfb) eight times (40 sts).
Row 9: purl.
Row 10: (k4, kfb) eight times (48 sts).
Rows 11–17: St st starting with a p row.
Row 18: (k4, k2tog) eight times (40 sts).
Row 19: purl.
Row 20: (k3, k2tog) eight times (32 sts).
Row 21: purl.
Row 22: (k2, k2tog) eight times (24 sts).
Row 23: purl.
Row 24: (k1, k2tog) eight times (16 sts).
Cast/bind off.

OUTER EAR (make two):
Using 5mm (UK 6; US 8) needles, cast on 24 sts in yarn A.
Rows 1 (WS)–3: St st starting with a p row.
Row 4: (k4, k2tog) four times (20 sts).
Rows 5-7: St st starting with a p row.
Row 8: (k3, k2tog) four times (16 sts).
Row 9: purl.
Row 10: (k2tog) eight times (8 sts).
Row 11: purl.
Break yarn and thread through rem sts, pull tight and fasten off securely.

INNER EAR (make two):
Using 5mm (UK 6; US 8) needles, cast on 20 sts in yarn B.
Rows 1 (WS)–3: St st starting with a p row.
Row 4: (k3, k2tog) four times (16 sts).
Row 5: purl.
Row 6: (k2, k2tog) four times (12 sts).
Row 7: purl.
Row 8: (k2tog) six times (6 sts).
Row 9: purl.
Break yarn and thread through rem sts, pull tight and fasten off securely.

ARM (make two):

Using 5mm (UK 6; US 8) needles, cast on 6 sts in yarn A.

Row 1 (WS): purl.
Row 2: (kfb) six times (12 sts).
Row 3: purl.
Row 4: (k1, kfb) six times (18 sts).
Row 5: purl.
Row 6: (k2, kfb) six times (24 sts).
Rows 7–9: St st starting with a p row.
Row 10: (k4, k2tog) four times (20 sts).
Rows 11–13: St st starting with a p row.
Row 14: (k3, k2tog) four times (16 sts).
Rows 15–17: St st starting with a p row.
Row 18: (k2, k2tog) four times (12 sts). Place marker here.
Rows 19–29: St st starting with a p row.
Row 30: k2tog, k8, k2tog (10 sts).
Rows 31–33: St st starting with a p row.
Row 34: k2tog, k6, k2tog (8 sts).
Row 35: purl.
Break yarn and thread through rem sts, pull tight and fasten off securely.

FRONT PAW (make two):

Using 5mm (UK 6; US 8) needles, cast on 12 sts in yarn A.

Row 1 (WS): purl.
Row 2: kfb, k10, kfb (14 sts).
Rows 3–5: St st starting with a p row.
Row 6: (k2tog) seven times (7 sts).
Row 7: purl.
Break yarn and thread through rem sts, pull tight and fasten off securely.

LEFT REAR LEG:

Using 5mm (UK 6; US 8) needles, cast on 6 sts in yarn A.

Row 1 (WS): purl.
Row 2: (kfb) six times (12 sts).
Row 3: purl.
Row 4: (k1, kfb) six times (18 sts).
Row 5: purl.
Row 6: (k2, kfb) six times (24 sts).
Row 7: purl.
Row 8: (k3, kfb) six times (30 sts).
Rows 9–17: St st starting with a p row.
Row 18: k2tog, k19, *turn*, leave rem 9 sts unworked (20 sts).
Row 19: purl.
Row 20: k2tog, k16, k2tog (18 sts).
Row 21: purl.
Row 22: k2tog, k14, k2tog (16 sts).
Row 23: purl.
Row 24: k2tog, k12, k2tog (14 sts).
Row 25: purl.
Row 26: (k2tog) seven times (7 sts).
Row 27: purl.
Break yarn and thread through rem sts, pull tight and fasten off securely.

Note: *this next section is working from the hip towards the foot, using the unworked stitches on Row 18.*
Row 1 (RS): working the 9 rem sts from Row 18, k9 sts (18 sts).
Rows 2–6: St st.
Row 7: (k2, kfb) six times (24 sts).
Row 8: purl.
Row 9: (k2, k2tog) six times (18 sts).
Row 10: purl.
Row 11: (k1, k2tog) six times (12 sts).
Break yarn and thread through rem sts, pull tight and fasten off securely.

RIGHT REAR LEG:

Using 5mm (UK 6; US 8) needles, cast on 6 sts in yarn A.

Row 1 (WS): purl.
Row 2: (kfb) six times (12 sts).
Row 3: purl.
Row 4: (k1, kfb) six times (18 sts).
Row 5: purl.
Row 6: (k2, kfb) six times (24 sts).
Row 7: purl.
Row 8: (k3, kfb) six times (30 sts).
Rows 9–17: St st starting with a p row.
Row 18: k9 and transfer these sts to a stitch holder, k19, k2tog (20 sts).
Row 19: purl.
Row 20: k2tog, k16, k2tog (18 sts).
Row 21: purl.
Row 22: k2tog, k14, k2tog (16 sts).
Row 23: purl.
Row 24: k2tog, k12, k2tog (14 sts).
Row 25: purl.
Row 26: (k2tog) seven times (7 sts).
Row 27: purl.
Break yarn and thread through rem sts, pull tight and fasten off securely.
Row 1 (WS): working the 9 rem sts from the stitch holder, p9 sts (18 sts).
Rows 2–5: St st starting with a knit row.
Row 6: (k2, kfb) six times (24 sts).
Row 7: purl.
Row 8: (k2, k2tog) six times (18 sts).
Row 9: purl.
Row 10: (k1, k2tog) six times (12 sts).
Row 11: purl.
Break yarn and thread through rem sts, pull tight and fasten off securely.

- TURNING YOUR KNITTING -

When you 'turn' your knitting, you are literally turning it part way through the row you are working on, before you have 'finished' the row. To continue you begin a new row, working on only the stitches you have knitted before the turn. This effect creates shape, and is something sock knitters use all the time.

STAGE 2: SEWING UP

1. With right sides facing, sew together the row ends of the body with yarn A, leaving a 4–5cm (1½–2in) gap in the middle for stuffing into later.

2. With right sides facing, sew together the row ends of the head with yarn A, leaving the cast-on edge open to create a rounded cup shape.

3. With the wrong sides facing, place the inner ear into the outer ear, as shown on the right. Carefully sew them in place with yarn B using small, close stitches.

4. With right sides facing, sew together the row ends of the arms between Rows 18 (marker) and 3 (the bottom paw part of the arm), using yarn A.

5. With right sides facing, fold over the paw sections of each sitting rear leg to form open cup shapes. Following the diagram, right, for the shape and indication of where to sew, use yarn A to sew together the row ends of each rear paw.

6. Sew together the row ends of the front paws with yarn A, leaving the cast-on edges open to create small cup shapes.

7. Fasten in all loose ends, as these can get in the way when felting. Turn all the hollow pieces the right way out.

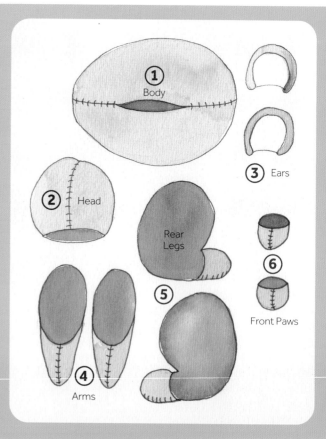

① Body

② Head

③ Ears

④ Arms

⑤ Rear Legs

⑥ Front Paws

STAGE 3: WET FELTING

1. Wet felt the body and head pieces for Twiglet, following the information on page 30.

2. Wet felt the remaining pieces, following the information on page 31.

3. When all pieces are felted equally, rinse them off. Pull the ears and legs of the rear legs into shape; the remaining hollow pieces (and paws of the rear legs) can be stuffed with kitchen roll.

4. Leave all pieces to dry completely.

STAGE 4: STUFFING & CONSTRUCTION

1. Stuff the body firmly and sew up the gap with yarn A.

2. Stuff the head and pin it into position, referring to the diagram. When you are happy with your positioning, sew the head to the body with yarn A using small, close stitches. Add extra stuffing before closing up the head completely, if required.

3. Stuff the front paws lightly then pin them into position at the closed, rounded ends of each arm, at a slight angle. Sew them in place with yarn A, using small, close stitches.

4. Stuff the arms firmly, then pin them into position onto each side of the body. Stuff the paws of the rear legs, too, then pin the rear legs into position. At this stage, take some time with the pinning process, to ensure Twiglet sits steadily on a flat surface. Once you are happy with the positions of the limbs, sew them in place with yarn A using small, close stitches. Add extra stuffing to the limbs before closing them up completely, especially in the 'hips'.

5. Position and pin the ears onto the upper sides of the head, as shown in the diagram. Sew the bases in place with yarn A.

STAGE 5: NEEDLE FELTING & DETAILS

1. Koalas have a fluffy appearance, so a layer of natural-grey wool roving makes a nice finish. Following the instructions on page 39, add a base layer of flat fur all over the body, head, the back of the ears and all the limbs using the grey wool roving. When adding the natural-grey to the back of the ears, trim your fibres a little longer than the ear edge for a fluffy edge. Remember to use a foam block or rice bag as you work this area, to protect your fingers and to provide a surface to work against.

2. Use natural white fleece to make Twiglet's fluffy white chest, following the instructions for short, tufty fur on page 42.

3. Using the natural white fleece again, follow the instructions on page 39 to add fur along the front crease of the rear legs, the back of the arms and front paws, the insides of the rear paws and over the inner ears. Secure the outer edges first of each shape then needle felt only here and there at the centre, to keep the shapes as fluffy as possible.

4. For the nose, create a large, firm, oval shape with the black merino wool tops by folding under the top and bottom edges of the strip of fibre and rolling the shape gently between your palms. Using the main picture on page 115 as a guide for placement, needle the nose into position: work around the outer edges first then lightly needle felt the middle here and there – you want to keep the shape as rounded and full at the centre as possible.

5. Repeat the technique of shaping the nose for the mouth piece, this time using a thin layer of natural white fleece. To finish the mouth, pull off a tiny, wispy amount of pink merino wool tops and needle felt this over the top section of the mouth.

6. Use the pink merino wool tops once again to make nostrils for Twiglet, following the Simple Nose instructions on page 53. Needle felt these onto the bottom section of the nose.

7. Create eye sockets for Twiglet, following the instructions on page 48.

8. Make detailed eyes for Twiglet, using the instructions on page 51: the order of merino wool tops colours, from base to top, is dark-brown, black then white.

9. To create the distinguished eyelids for Twiglet, 'draw' twisted white merino tops around each eye and needle felt them in place, following the Linear Details instructions on page 54.

10. Use the small amount of dark grey yarn to sew the digits onto the front and back paws of Twiglet, following the instructions on page 56.

MARMALADE THE CAT & PUMPKIN THE KITTEN

Pumpkin is the super-cheeky, adorable son to his mother, Marmalade.
Both are knitted using aran (worsted) weight yarn, and are detailed with
subtle-coloured wool tops to create beautifully realistic ginger cats.
Pumpkin is a purr-fect mini project to get you started, before making
Marmalade to complete this fabulous, feline family.

Difficulty

• Intermediate

What you need

• Yarn
▷ *200g (7oz) of Drops Alaska in Mustard, or equivalent aran (worsted) weight
100% pure wool yarn in mustard; 50g/77yd/70m* **[A]**
▷ *70g (2½oz) of Drops Alaska in Off White, or equivalent aran (worsted) weight
100% pure wool yarn in off-white; 50g/77yd/70m* **[B]**

• Felting fibres
▷ *Mustard, white, black, red-brown, dark pink, blue and moss-green merino
wool tops*

• Toy filling

• Stitch marker (a contrasting-coloured scrap of yarn makes a
handy, economical alternative)

Needles

• One pair of 5mm (UK 6; US 8) needles
• Tapestry needle
• Set of three needle-felting needles in sizes 40, 38 and 32

Tension/gauge

• 17 sts x 22 rows in a 10cm (4in) square over St st,
using 5mm (UK 6; US 8) needles

INSTRUCTIONS

STAGE 1: THE KNIT BIT

Pumpkin the Kitten

BODY:
Using 5mm (UK 6; US 8) needles, cast on 6 sts in yarn A.
Row 1 (RS): (kfb) six times (12 sts).
Row 2: purl.
Row 3: (k1, kfb) six times (18 sts).
Row 4: purl.
Row 5: (k2, kfb) six times (24 sts).
Row 6: purl.
Row 7: (k3, kfb) six times (30 sts).
Row 8: purl.
Row 9: (k4, kfb) six times (36 sts).
Row 10: purl.
Row 11: (k5, kfb) six times (42 sts).
Rows 12-14: St st.
Row 15: (k5, k2tog) six times (36 sts).
Rows 16-24: St st.
Row 25: (k4, k2tog) six times (30 sts).
Row 26. purl.
Row 27: (k3, k2tog) six times (24 sts).
Row 28: purl.
Row 29: (k2, k2tog) six times (18 sts).
Row 30: purl.
Row 31: (k1, k2tog) six times (12 sts).
Row 32: purl.
Row 33: (k2tog) six times (6 sts).
Break yarn and thread through rem sts, pull tight and fasten off securely.

MUZZLE:
Using 5mm (UK 6; US 8) needles, cast on 12 sts in yarn B.
Rows 1 (WS)-3: St st starting with a p row.
Row 4: (k2tog) six times (6 sts).
Break yarn and thread through rem sts, pull tight and fasten off securely.

EARS (make two):
Using 5mm (UK 6; US 8) needles, cast on 6 sts in yarn A.
Row 1 (RS): knit.
Row 2: purl.
Row 3: k2, k2tog, k2 (5 sts).
Row 4: purl.
Row 5: k2tog, k1, k2tog (3 sts).
Break yarn and thread through rem sts, pull tight and fasten off securely.

HEAD:
Using 5mm (UK 6; US 8) needles, cast on 20 sts in yarn A.
Row 1 (WS): purl.
Row 2: (k3, kfb) five times (25 sts).
Row 3: purl.
Row 4: (k4, kfb) five times (30 sts).
Row 5-7: St st starting with a p row.
Row 8: (k4, k2tog) five times (25 sts).
Row 9: purl.
Row 10: (k3, k2tog) five times (20 sts).
Row 11: purl.
Row 12: (k2, k2tog) five times (15 sts).
Row 13: purl.
Row 14: (k1 k2tog) five times (10 sts).
Row 15: purl.
Break yarn and thread through rem sts, pull tight and fasten off securely.

REAR LEG (make two):
Using 5mm (UK 6; US 8) needles, cast on 16 sts in yarn A.
Rows 1 (WS)-3: St st starting with a p row.
Row 4: (k2, k2tog) four times (12 sts).
Row 5: purl.
Change to yarn B.
Row 6: k9, *turn.*
Row 7: p6, *turn.*
Row 8: k5, k2tog, *turn.*
Row 9: p5, p2tog, *turn.*
Rows 10-13: rep last 2 rows twice more (6 sts).

Rows 14-17: St st.
Row 18: k2tog, k2, k2tog (4 sts).
Row 19: purl.
Row 20: (k2tog) twice (2 sts).
Row 21: purl.
Break yarn and thread through rem sts, pull tight and fasten off securely.

FRONT LEG (make two):
Using 5mm (UK 6; US 8) needles, cast on 12 sts in yarn A.
Rows 1 (WS)-3: St st starting with a p row.
Row 4: k2tog, k8, k2tog (10 sts).
Rows 5-7: St st starting with a p row.
Change to yarn B.
Row 8: k8, *turn.*
Row 9: p6, *turn.*
Row 10: k5, k2tog, *turn.*
Row 11: p5, p2tog, *turn.*
Rows 12 and 13: rep last 2 rows twice more (6 sts).
Rows 14 and 15: St st.
Row 16: k2tog, k2, k2tog (4 sts).
Row 17: purl.
Row 18: (k2tog) twice (2 sts).
Row 19: purl.
Break yarn and thread through rem sts, pull tight and fasten off securely.

TAIL:
Using 5mm (UK 6; US 8) needles, cast on 10 sts in yarn A.
Rows 1 (WS)-7: St st starting with a p row.
Row 8: k2tog, k6, k2tog (8 sts).
Row 9: purl.
Row 10: k2tog, k4, k2tog (6 sts).
Rows 11: purl.
Row 12: k2tog, k2, k2tog (4 sts).
Row 13: purl.
Row 14: (k2tog) twice (2 sts).
Break yarn and thread through rem sts, pull tight and fasten off securely.

STAGE 2: SEWING UP

Pumpkin the Kitten

1. With right sides facing, sew together the row ends of the body with yarn A, leaving a 4–5cm (1½–2in) gap in the middle for stuffing into later.

2. With right sides facing, sew together the row ends of the head with yarn A, leaving the cast-on edges open to create a small cup shape.

3. With right sides facing, sew together the row ends of the muzzle with yarn B, leaving the cast-on edges open to create a tiny cup shape.

4. With right sides facing, sew up the front and rear legs with matching yarn, using the diagram, right, and the instructions on page 26 to help you: fold the leg in half from the point of the toe, turn in the toe and sew up the length of the leg and each side of the toe as indicated, alternating between yarns A and B.

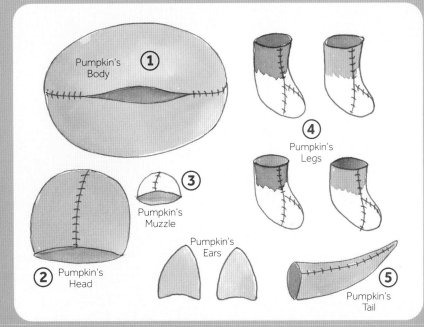

5. With right sides facing, sew together the row ends of the tail with yarn A, working towards the point and leaving the cast-on edge open.

6. Fasten in all loose ends as these can get in the way when felting. Turn all the hollow pieces the right way out.

Marmalade the Cat

BODY & HEAD:
Using 5mm (UK 6; US 8) needles, cast on 6 sts in yarn A.
Row 1 (WS), 3, 5, 7: purl.
Row 2: (kfb) six times (12 sts).
Row 4: (kfb) twelve times (24 sts).
Row 6: (k1, kfb) twelve times (36 sts).
Row 8: (k2, kfb) twelve times (48 sts).
Rows 9–11: St st starting with a p row.
Row 12: (k3, kfb) twelve times (60 sts).
Rows 13–23: St st starting with a p row.
Row 24: (k4, k2tog) ten times (50 sts).
Rows 25–35: St st starting with a p row.
Row 36: k15, k2tog, k16, k2tog, k15 (48 sts).
Rows 37–47: St st starting with a p row.
Row 48: (k4, k2tog) eight times (40 sts).
Rows 49–53: St st starting with a p row.
Row 54: (k2tog) twenty times (20 sts).
Rows 55–57: St st starting with a p row.
Row 58: (k1, kfb) ten times (30 sts).
Row 59: purl.
Row 60: (k5, kfb) five times (35 sts).
Row 61: purl.
Row 62: (k4, kfb) seven times (42 sts).
Rows 63–73: St st starting with a p row.
Row 74: (k5, k2tog) six times (36 sts).
Row 75: purl.
Row 76: (k4, k2tog) six times (30 sts).
Row 77: purl.
Row 78: (k1, k2tog) ten times (20 sts).
Row 79: purl.
Row 80: (k2tog) ten times (10 sts).
Break yarn and thread through rem sts, pull tight and fasten off securely.

EAR (make two):
Using 5mm (UK 6; US 8) needles, cast on 9 sts in yarn A.
Rows 1 (WS)–3: St st starting with a p row.
Row 4: k2tog, k5, k2tog (7 sts).
Row 5: purl.
Row 6: k2tog, k3, k2tog (5 sts).
Row 7: purl.
Row 8: k2tog, k1, k2tog (3 sts).
Break yarn and thread through rem sts, pull tight and fasten off securely.

NOSE:
Using 5mm (UK 6; US 8) needles, cast on 20 sts in yarn B.
Rows 1 (WS)–3: St st starting with a p row.
Row 4: (k3, k2tog) four times (16 sts).
Row 5: purl.
Row 6: (k2tog) eight times (8 sts).
Break yarn and thread through rem sts, pull tight and fasten off securely.

FRONT LEG (make two):
Using 5mm (UK 6; US 8) needles, cast on 6 sts in yarn A.
Rows 1 (WS)–5: St st starting with a p row.
Row 6: kfb, k4, kfb (8 sts).
Row 7: purl.
Row 8: kfb, k6, kfb (10 sts).
Row 9: purl.
Row 10: kfb, k8, kfb (12 sts).
Row 11: purl.
Row 12: kfb, k10, kfb (14 sts).
Row 13: purl.
Row 14: kfb, k12, kfb (16 sts). Place a stitch marker here.
Rows 15–21: St st starting with a p row.
Row 22: k2tog, k12, k2tog (14 sts).
Row 23: purl.
Row 24: k2tog, k10, k2tog (12 sts).
Rows 25–29: St st starting with a p row.
Row 30: (k2tog) six times (6 sts).
Break yarn and thread through rem sts, pull tight and fasten off securely.

FRONT PAW (make two):
Using 5mm (UK 6; US 8) needles, cast on 14 sts in yarn B.
Rows 1 (WS)–4: St st starting with a p row.
Row 5: (p2tog) seven times.
Break yarn and thread through rem sts, pull tight and fasten off securely.

REAR LEFT LEG:
Using 5mm (UK 6; US 8) needles, cast on 7 sts in yarn A.
Row 1 (WS): purl.
Row 2: (kfb) seven times (14 sts).
Row 3: purl.
Row 4: kfb, k12, kfb (16 sts).
Row 5: purl.
Row 6: kfb, k14, kfb (18 sts).
Rows 7–11: St st starting with a p row.
Row 12: k2tog, k to end (17 sts).
Row 13: p to last 2 sts, p2tog (16 sts).
Row 14: k2tog, k to end (15 sts).
Row 15: p to last 2 sts, p2tog (14 sts).
Row 16: k2tog, k to end (13 sts).
Row 17: p to last 2 sts, p2tog (12 sts).
Row 18: k2tog, k to end (11 sts).
Row 19: p to last 2 sts, p2tog (10 sts).
Row 20: cast off 4 sts, k to end (6 sts).
Change to yarn B.
Row 21: purl.
Row 22: cast on 6 sts, k to end (12 sts).
Rows 23–27: St st starting with a p row.

Row 28: (k1, k2tog) four times (8 sts).
Row 29: purl.
Row 30: (k2tog) four times (4 sts).
Break yarn and thread through rem sts, pull tight and fasten off securely.

REAR LEFT LEG:
Using 5mm (UK 6; US 8) needles, cast on 7 sts in yarn A.
Row 1 (WS): purl.
Row 2: (kfb) seven times (14 sts).
Row 3: purl.
Row 4: kfb, k12, kfb (16 sts).
Row 5: purl.
Row 6: kfb, k14, kfb (18 sts).
Rows 7–11: St st starting with a p row.
Row 12: k to last 2 sts, k2tog (17 sts).
Row 13: p2tog, p to end (16 sts).

Row 14: k to last 2 sts, k2tog (15 sts).
Row 15: p2tog, p to end (14 sts).
Row 16: k to last 2 sts, k2tog (13 sts).
Row 17: p2tog, p to end (12 sts).
Row 18: k to last 2 sts, k2tog (11 sts).
Row 19: p2tog, p to end (10 sts).
Row 20: k6, cast off 4 sts, break yarn and thread through last st (6 sts).
Change to yarn B.
Row 21: purl.
Row 22: knit.
Row 23: cast on 6 sts, p to end (12 sts).
Rows 24–27: St st.
Row 28: (k1, k2tog) four times (8 sts).
Row 29: purl.
Row 30: (k2tog) four times (4 sts).
Break yarn and thread through rem sts, pull tight and fasten off securely.

TAIL:
Using 5mm (UK 6; US 8) needles, cast on 16 sts in yarn A.
Rows 1 (WS)–13: St st starting with a p row.
Row 14: k2tog, k12, k2tog (14 sts).
Rows 15–27: St st starting with a p row.
Row 28: k2tog, k10, k2tog (12 sts).
Rows 29–35: St st starting with a p row.
Row 36: k2tog, k8, k2tog (10 sts).
Rows 37–39: St st starting with a p row.
Row 40: k2tog, k6, k2tog (8 sts).
Rows 41–43: St st starting with a p row.
Row 44: (k2tog) four times (4 sts).
Break yarn and thread through rem sts, pull tight and fasten off securely.

STAGE 2: SEWING UP

Marmalade the Cat

1. With right sides facing, sew together the row ends of the body, with yarn A leaving a 4–5cm (1½–2in) gap in the middle for stuffing into later.

2. With right sides facing, sew together the row ends of the muzzle with yarn B, leaving the cast-on edge open to create a small cup shape.

3. With right sides facing, sew together the row ends of each front paw with yarn B, leaving the cast-on edges open to create tiny cup shapes.

4. With right sides facing, sew together the row ends of each of the front legs with yarn A, leaving the cast-on edges open. Note that the 'back' of each front leg is slightly longer than the sewn-up section; this is correct.

5. With right sides facing, fold over the smaller 'foot' sections of each sitting rear leg to form open cup shapes. Following the diagram right for the shape and indication of where to sew, use yarn A to sew together the row ends of each foot.

6. With right sides facing, sew together the row ends of the tail with yarn A, working from the cast-on edge towards the point. Leave the cast-on edge open.

7. Fasten in all loose ends as these can get in the way when felting. Turn all the pieces the right way out.

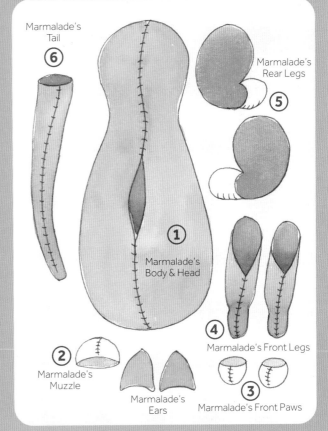

Marmalade's Tail
⑥

Marmalade's Rear Legs
⑤

Marmalade's Body & Head
①

Marmalade's Muzzle
②

Marmalade's Ears

Marmalade's Front Legs
④

Marmalade's Front Paws
③

STAGE 3: WET FELTING

1. Wet felt the head and body pieces for Pumpkin, and the body piece for Marmalade, following the information on page 30.

2. Wet felt the remaining pieces for both Pumpkin and Marmalade, following the information on page 31.

3. When all the pieces are felted equally, rinse them off. Pull the ears of both Pumpkin and Marmalade into shape; the remaining hollow pieces (and the paws of the rear legs of Marmalade) can be stuffed with kitchen roll.

4. Leave all the pieces to dry completely.

STAGE 4: STUFFING & CONSTRUCTION

Pumpkin the Kitten

1. Stuff the body firmly then sew up the gap in the tummy with yarn A.

2. Stuff the head and pin it into position on the body, referring to the diagram. When you are happy with your positioning, sew the head to the body with yarn A, using small, close stitches. Add extra stuffing before completely closing up, if required.

3. Stuff the muzzle and pin it into position onto the head – the seam edge should be facing down. When you are happy with your positioning, sew the muzzle in place with yarn B using small, close stitches. Add extra stuffing before completely closing up, if required.

4. Stuff the legs then pin them onto the body as shown in the diagram. Take some time with the pinning process, to ensure Pumpkin stands steadily on a flat surface. Once you are happy with their positioning, sew each leg in place. Add more stuffing before completely sewing on the legs, if required.

5. Pin the ears into position on top of the head so that the hollows of the ears are facing forwards, then sew the bases in place with yarn A.

6. Stuff the tail then pin it into position at the back of the body. Sew in place with yarn A, using small, close stitches.

STAGE 4: STUFFING & CONSTRUCTION

Marmalade the Cat

1. Stuff the body firmly then sew up the gap in the tummy with yarn A.

2. Stuff the muzzle then pin it into position on the body – the seam edge should be facing down. When you are happy with your positioning, sew the muzzle in place with yarn B using small, close stitches. Add extra stuffing before completely closing up, if required.

3. Stuff the paws lightly then pin them into position onto the closed, rounded ends of the front legs, at a slight angle. Sew them in place with yarn B, using small, close stitches.

4. Stuff the front legs and pin them onto the front of the body. Stuff the 'foot' of each rear leg then pin the rear legs onto each side of the body. Take some time with the pinning process, to ensure Marmalade sits steadily on a flat surface. Once you are happy with their positioning, sew the legs in place. Add more stuffing before completely sewing up the limbs, especially in the 'hips' of the rear legs.

5. Pin the ears into position on top of the head so that the hollows of the ears are facing forwards, then sew the ears in place with yarn A.

6. Stuff the tail then pin it into position at the back of the body. Sew in place with yarn A using small, close stitches.

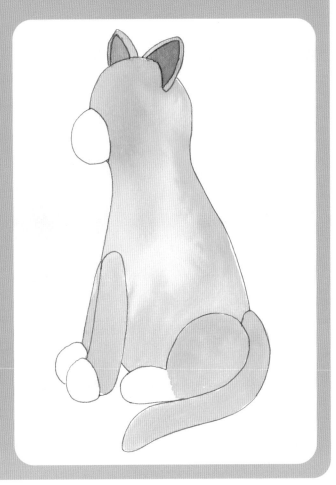

STAGE 5: NEEDLE FELTING & DETAILS

Pumpkin the Kitten

1. To hide any seams and to provide a surface for your markings later, lay a base layer of flat fur all over the body, head, top of the legs, tail and ears, following the instructions on page 39 and using mustard merino wool tops.

2. With two small lengths of dark-pink merino wool tops, add the inner ear shading to each ear, following the instructions on page 54.

3. Make the cheeks for Pumpkin with the white merino wool tops, following the instructions on page 49.

4. Sculpt the nose with the mustard merino wool tops, referring to the instructions on page 50.

5. Make detailed eyes for Pumpkin, using the instructions on page 51 as a guide: the order of merino wool tops colours, from base to top, is black, blue, black then white.

6. Add eyebrows, following the instructions on page 52.

7. Add a shaped nose with the dark-pink merino wool tops, following the instructions on page 53.

8. 'Draw' the lines of the mouth with twisted dark-pink merino wool tops, following the Linear Details instructions on page 54.

9. Referring to the instructions on page 44, add markings all over Pumpkin's body using a combination of white and red-brown merino wool tops. For Pumpkin's body I have added only white stripes; on the head, I have laid a white stripe on the back on the head and on the forehead, then defined the white stripe on the forehead with a stripe of red-brown on each side. Leave the ends of these head marking fibres loose to make a tufty effect.

10. Using the Colour Blending instructions on pages 46 and 47 as a guide, finish off Pumpkin's head by needle felting small, folded lengths of tufty hair to each side of the face, using a combination of white and mustard merino wool tops.

11. Add fluffy fur around Pumpkin's tummy and bottom with the white merino wool tops, following the Short, Tufty Fur instructions on page 42. Follow the technique for fluffy fur on page 41 to fluff some of the mustard fibres around the tummy and bottom.

12. To add fluff to the tail, layer a small amount of mustard merino wool tops over a small amount of white merino wool tops, then 'wrap' these layers around the length of the tail. Needle felt them in place around the top and sides of the tail – remember to use a foam block or rice bag when you do this, to protect your fingers. Once the fibres are secure on top, trim the merino wool tops on the underside.

13. Pull your felting needle through the longer fibres on the face, belly, bottom and tail, to feather them further and give Pumpkin's fur a natural finish.

Marmalade the Cat

1. To hide any seams and to provide a surface for markings, lay a base layer of flat fur all over the body, head, top of the legs, tail and ears, following the instructions on page 39 and using the mustard merino wool tops.

2. With two small lengths of red-brown merino wool tops, add the inner ear shading to each ear, following the instructions on page 54.

3. Sculpt the eye sockets, following the instructions on page 48.

4. Make the cheeks for Marmalade with the white merino wool tops, following the instructions on page 49.

5. Sculpt the nose with the mustard merino wool tops, referring to the instructions on page 50.

6. Make detailed eyes for Pumpkin, using the instructions on page 51 as a guide: the order of merino wool tops colours, from base to top, is black, moss-green, black then white.

7. Add eyebrows, following the instructions on page 52.

8. Add a shaped nose with the dark-pink merino wool tops, following the instructions on page 53.

9. Using the black merino wool tops, make nostrils for Marmalade following the Simple Nose instructions on page 53.

10. 'Draw' the lines of the mouth with twisted dark-pink merino wool tops, following the Linear Details instructions on page 54.

11. Referring to the instructions on page 44, add markings all over Marmalade's body using a combination of white and red-brown merino wool tops. For Marmalade's body and tail I have added only white stripes; on the legs and head I have used a combination of red-brown and white stripes.

12. Finish off Marmalade's head by needle felting small, amounts of white merino wool tops to each side of the face, following the Short, Tufty Fur instructions on page 42.

13. Add fluffy fur to Marmalade's chest, tummy, and tail tip with the white merino wool tops, referring to the Short, Tufty Fur instructions on page 42.

14. Following the Long Fur instructions on page 43, add tufty fur to the front paws, using a combination of the mustard and white merino wool tops. Trim the fibres right down to make the fur on the paws relatively short.

15. Sew the inner front paws together, using yarn A. Secure the tail to the side of one rear leg with a few anchor stitches, again using yarn A.

HEATH & BROOK
THE OWLS

Here we have Heath and Brook, perching companionably as they often do. Both are made with the same pattern, which shows you how using different-coloured yarns makes it possible to create two different looks. Heath is knitted using off-white yarn to make a snowy owl, whilst Brook is knitted using grey yarn to create a lovely, handsome, speckled-grey owl. The main differences come through the needle-felted detailing at the end.

Difficulty

- Intermediate

What you need

- **Yarn**
  ▷ *100g (3½oz) of Drops Alaska in Off White* **OR** *Drops Alaska in Light Brown Mix, or equivalent aran (worsted) weight 100% pure wool yarn in off-white* **OR** *variegated grey-brown; 50g/77yd/70m* **[A]**
  ▷ *20g (¾oz) of Drops Alaska in Pearl Grey Mix, or equivalent aran (worsted) weight 100% pure wool yarn in variegated light-grey; 50g/77yd/70m* **[B]**
  ▷ *20g (¾oz) of Drops Alaska in Dark Grey Mix, or equivalent aran (worsted) weight 100% pure wool yarn in variegated dark grey-brown; 50g/77yd/70m* **[C]**
- **Felting fibres**
  ▷ *Gold, white and black merino wool tops*
  ▷ *Light-grey and grey-brown wool roving*
  ▷ *Natural white fleece*
- **Toy filling**
- Stitch marker (a contrasting-coloured scrap of yarn makes a handy, economical alternative)

Needles

- One pair of 5mm (UK 6; US 8) needles
- Tapestry needle
- Set of three needle-felting needles in sizes 40, 38 and 32

Tension/gauge

- 18 sts x 24 rows in a 10cm (4in) square over St st, using 5mm (UK 6; US 8) needles

INSTRUCTIONS

STAGE 1: THE KNIT BIT

BODY & HEAD:
Using 5mm (UK 6; US 8) needles, cast on 6 sts in yarn A.
Rows 1 (WS), 3, 5, 7: purl.
Row 2: (kfb) six times (12 sts).
Row 4: (kfb) twelve times (24 sts).
Row 6: (k1, kfb) twelve times (36 sts).
Row 8: (k2, kfb) twelve times (48 sts).
Rows 9–11: St st starting with a p row.
Row 12: (k3, kfb) twelve times (60 sts).
Rows 13–47: St st starting with a p row.
Row 48: (k2tog) to end (30 sts).
Row 49: purl.
Row 50: (k2, kfb) ten times (40 sts).
Row 51: purl.
Row 52: (k7, kfb) five times (45 sts).
Rows 53–65: St st starting with a p row.
Row 66: (k3, k2tog) nine times (36 sts).
Row 67: purl.
Row 68: (k2, k2tog) nine times (27 sts).
Row 69: purl.
Row 70: (k1, k2tog) nine times (18 sts).
Rows 71–73: St st starting with a p row.
Row 74: (k2tog) nine times (9 sts).
Row 75: purl.
Break yarn and thread through rem sts, pull tight and fasten off securely.

WING (make two):
Using 5mm (UK 6; US 8) needles, cast on 6 sts in yarn A.
Row 1 (WS): purl.
Row 2: (kfb) six times (12 sts).
Row 3: purl.
Row 4: (k1, kfb) six times (18 sts).
Row 5: purl.
Row 6: (k2, kfb) six times (24 sts).
Rows 7–13: St st starting with a p row.
Row 14: (k3, kfb) six times (30 sts).
Rows 15–17: St st starting with a p row.
Row 18: (k3, k2tog) six times (24 sts).
Rows 19–25: St st starting with a p row.
Row 26: (k2, k2tog) six times (18 sts).
Rows 27–31: St st starting with a p row.
Row 32: (k1, k2tog) six times (12 sts).
Rows 33–39: St st starting with a p row.
Row 40: (k1, k2tog) four times (8 sts).
Rows 41–43: St st starting with a p row.
Row 44: (k2tog) four times (4 sts).

Row 45: purl.
Row 46: (k2tog) twice (2 sts).
Row 47: purl.
Row 48: k2tog (1 st).
Break yarn and thread through rem sts, pull tight and fasten off securely.

TAIL:
Using 5mm (UK 6; US 8) needles, cast on 10 sts in yarn A.
Row 1 (WS): purl.
Row 2: kfb, k to last st, kfb (12 sts).
Row 3: purl.
Row 4: kfb, k to last st, kfb (14 sts).
Row 5: purl.
Row 6: kfb, k to last st, kfb (16 sts).
Rows 7–15: St st starting with a p row.
Row 16: k2tog, k to last 2 sts, k2tog (14 sts).
Row 17: purl.
Rows 18–29: rep rows 16 and 17 until 2 sts rem.
Break yarn and thread through rem sts, pull tight and secure.

FOOT (make two):
Using 5mm (UK 6; US 8) needles, cast on 24 sts in yarn B for Heath; use yarn C for Brook.
Rows 1 (WS)–5: St st starting with a p row.
Cast/bind off.

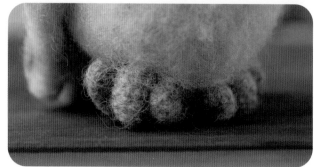

STAGE 2: SEWING UP

1. With right sides facing, sew together the row ends of the body & head with matching yarn, leaving a 5–6cm (2–2½in) gap in the middle for stuffing into later.

2. Fasten in the loose ends as these can get in the way when felting. Turn the body the right way out.

STAGE 3: WET FELTING

1. Wet felt the body following the information on page 30.

2. Wet felt the wings and tail following the information on page 31.

3. When felting the feet, roll the knitted shapes between the palms of your hands to create tubular shapes.

4. When all the pieces are felted equally, rinse them off. Pull the wings and tail into shape – with the tail, ensure that the wider bottom edge is turned upwards slightly. Leave the feet untouched. The remaining body & head piece can be stuffed with kitchen roll.

5. Leave all the pieces to dry completely.

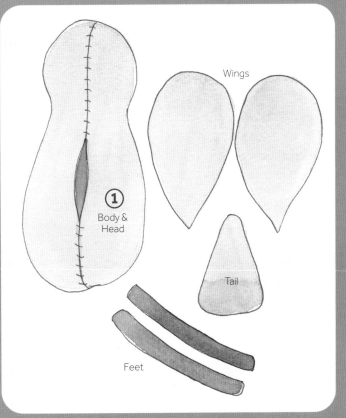

STAGE 4: STUFFING & CONSTRUCTION

1. Stuff the body & head, shaping the sections as you work. Sew up the gap in the tummy with matching yarn.

2. Position and pin the wings onto each side of the body, as shown in the diagram. Sew in place with matching yarn.

3. Position and pin the tail piece onto the body – the flicked-up end should be at the bottom. The tail should also extend beyond the bottom of the body.

4. Fold and squidge together each of the tubular shapes for the feet as indicated in the diagram, right. Using matching yarn, take the needle from one side of the foot, through the folds and out of the other side of the foot. Repeat once again, from the opposite side, then pull to hold the 'W' shape of the foot in place. Fasten off.

5. Position and pin the feet onto the base of the body.

6. Take the time to reposition the feet and tail, if needed, to ensure that the owl stands up steadily. Once you are happy with their positioning, sew the tail and feet to the body using matching yarn.

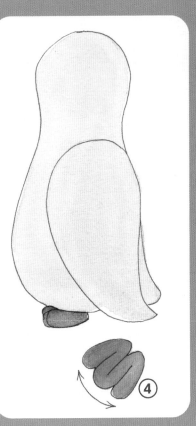

STAGE 5: NEEDLE FELTING & DETAILS

Heath (the snowy owl)

1. Use the natural white fleece to add a base layer of flat fur all over the head, body, wings and tail, following the instructions on page 39. Referring to the information on page 41, flick the felting needle all over the base fur to make it tufty.

2. Make detailed eyes for Heath, using the instructions on page 51 as a guide: the order of merino wool tops colours, from base to top, is black, gold then white. Note that I have positioned the face and eyes to the side, to suggest the famous, extensive head swivel of an owl!

3. You need to build raised sections on the face which run around the eyes and along the top of the beak – these add shape to the eye area and make the eyes more almond shaped and owl-like. Using 5–6cm (2–2¼in) lengths of natural white fleece, needle felt eyebrows onto Heath's face, following steps 1 and 2 in the instructions on page 52. Leave the ends of the eyebrows loose to add a fluffy texture.

4. Pull and roll another 5–6cm (2–2¼in) length of natural white fleece and make this into a 'moustache' shape. Place this just below the eyes then needle felt it in place, starting from the centre and working your way outwards. Leave the ends loose to add a fluffy texture.

5. To make the beak, gently roll a pea-sized ball of the black merino wool tops and then gently roll it sideways to make a tear-drop shape. Centre it over the face, below the eyes, and needle felt it into place – work around the edges mostly, leaving the centre relatively unfelted to keep the shape rounded.

6. To add feather markings, pull off a thin length of light-grey wool roving and gently open out the fibres to make a flat piece that is 1–2cm (⅜–¾in) wide. Lay the piece onto the back of the body and needle felt along the width only, 1cm (⅜in) down from the top. Trim 1cm (⅜in) down from the needle-felted middle and put the excess aside. Fold the top section down, and use the point of your needle to stroke the fibres down.

7. Repeat with the remaining and additional lengths of opened-out light-grey wool roving, to add more markings to the wings, back of the body, tail and head.

Brook (the grey barn owl)

1. Use the grey-brown wool roving to add a base layer of flat fur all over the head, body, wings and tail, following the instructions on page 39.

2. Over the chest and tummy, between the wings and right down to the feet, add a thin layer of natural white fleece. Shape the top slightly, ensuring that there is a clean, slightly arched top edge that smoothly touches the sides of the wings.

3. Shape a thin piece of natural white fleece into a large, slightly heart-shaped circle, then needle felt this over the head to begin making Brook's face – note that I have positioned the face to the side, as for Heath.

4. Follow the information in step 2 for Heath, left, to add Brook's eyes. Note that the pupils for Brook have been manipulated further, to create stronger points at each end. Referring to the Linear Details instructions on page 54, twist two lengths of grey-brown roving and needle felt one under each eye, to frame them further.

5. Use the natural white fleece to add eyebrows and the top of the beak to Brook's face, following the instructions in steps 1 and 2 on page 52.

6. To make the beak, gently roll a pea-sized ball of the gold merino wool tops and then gently roll the ball sideways to make a tear-drop shape. Centre it over the face, below the eyes, and needle felt the beak into place – work around the edges mostly, leaving the centre relatively unfelted to keep the shape rounded.

7. To add feather markings, pull off very small pieces of natural fleece and lay each one at random onto the wings, back, head and tail. Needle felt them flat to the surface.

- TIP -

Have fun customizing your owl even more! Take a look at photographs in magazines, books and online, to see what other owl species you can recreate in wool and felt. For example, why not use the Colour Blending technique on pages 46 and 47 to make little tufty ears, then build up the area between the eyes with rolled fibres, to make an eagle owl?

EMBER THE FOX

Ember is a clever-looking little chap and would look lovely on any bookshelf or mantle piece. He is knitted using double-knit (light worsted) yarn, so that finer features are possible – ideal for creating the slim features of the fox.

Difficulty

• Intermediate to Difficult

What you need

• Yarn

▷ 80g (3oz) of Woolyknit DK Classics in Rust, or equivalent DK (light worsted) weight 100% pure wool yarn in red-brown; 50g/106yd/96m [A]
▷ Small amount of black or charcoal yarn, for sewing the toes

• Felting fibres

▷ Ready-blended mustard-mix, white, brown and black merino wool tops
▷ Charcoal wool roving
▷ Natural white fleece

• Toy filling

• Stitch holder

• Stitch marker (a contrasting-coloured scrap of yarn makes a handy, economical alternative)

Needles

• One pair of 4mm (UK 8; US 6) needles
• Tapestry needle
• Set of three needle-felting needles in sizes 40, 38 and 32

Tension/gauge

• 22 sts x 28 rows in a 10cm (4in) square over St st, using 4mm (UK 8; US 6) needles

INSTRUCTIONS

STAGE 1: THE KNIT BIT

BODY:
Using 4mm (UK 8; US 6) needles, cast on 6 sts in yarn A.
Row 1 (WS): purl.
Row 2: (kfb) six times (12 sts).
Row 3: purl.
Row 4: (k1, kfb) six times (18 sts).
Row 5: purl.
Row 6: (k2, kfb) six times (24 sts).
Row 7: purl.
Row 8: (k3, kfb) six times (30 sts).
Row 9: purl.
Row 10: (k2, kfb) ten times (40 sts).
Rows 11–19: St st starting with a p row.
Row 20: (k7, kfb) five times (45 sts).
Rows 21–29: St st starting with a p row.
Row 30: (k8, kfb) five times (50 sts).
Rows 31–43: St st starting with a p row.
Row 44: (k8, k2tog) five times (45 sts).
Row 45: purl.
Row 46: (k7, k2tog) five times (40 sts).
Row 47: purl.
Row 48: (k6, k2tog) five times (35 sts).
Row 49: purl.
Row 50: (k5, k2tog) five times (30 sts).
Row 51: purl.
Row 52: (k3, k2tog) six times (24 sts).
Row 53: purl.
Row 54: (k2, k2tog) six times (18 sts).
Row 55: purl.
Row 56: (k1, k2tog) six times (12 sts).
Row 57: purl.
Row 58: (k2tog) six times (6 sts).
Break yarn and thread through rem sts, pull tight and fasten off securely.

HEAD:
Using 4mm (UK 8; US 6) needles, cast on 30 sts in yarn A.
Rows 1 (WS)–9: St st starting with a p row.
Row 10: (k5, kfb) five times (35 sts).
Rows 11–23: St st starting with a p row.
Row 24: (k5, k2tog) five times (30 sts).
Row 25: purl.
Row 26: (k4, k2tog) five times (25 sts).
Row 27: purl.
Row 28: (k3, k2tog) five times (20 sts).

Row 29: purl.
Row 30: (k2, k2tog) five times (15 sts).
Row 31: purl.
Row 32: (k1, k2tog) five times (10 sts).
Row 33: purl.
Break yarn and thread through rem sts, pull tight and fasten off securely.

MUZZLE:
Using 4mm (UK 8; US 6) needles, cast on 20 sts in yarn A.
Rows 1 (WS)–3: St st starting with a p row.
Row 4: (k3, k2tog) four times (16 sts).
Rows 5–7: St st starting with a p row.
Row 8: k2tog, k12, k2tog (14 sts).
Row 9: purl.
Row 10: k2tog, k10, k2tog (12 sts).
Row 11: purl.
Row 12: k2tog, k8, k2tog (10 sts).
Row 13: purl.
Row 14: k2tog, k6, k2tog (8 sts).
Break yarn and thread through rem sts, pull tight and fasten off securely.

EAR (make two):
Using 4mm (UK 8; US 6) needles, cast on 10 sts in yarn A.
Rows 1 (WS)–5: St st starting with a p row.
Row 6: k2tog, k6, k2tog (8 sts).
Rows 7–9: St st starting with a p row.
Row 10: k2tog, k4, k2tog (6 sts).
Row 11: purl.
Row 12: k2tog, k2, k2tog (4 sts).
Row 13: purl.
Row 14: (k2tog) twice (2 sts).
Row 15: purl.
Break yarn and thread through rem sts, pull tight and fasten off securely.

TAIL:
Using 4mm (UK 8; US 6) needles, cast on 14 sts in yarn A.
Rows 1 (WS)–5: St st starting with a p row.
Row 6: kfb, k12, kfb (16 sts).
Rows 7–37: St st starting with a p row.
Row 38: k2tog, k12, k2tog (14 sts).
Row 39: purl.
Row 40: k2tog, k10, k2tog (12 sts).
Row 41: purl.

Row 42: (k2, k2tog) three times (9 sts).
Row 43: purl.
Row 44: (k1, k2tog) three times (6 sts).
Break yarn and thread through rem sts, pull tight and fasten off securely.

FRONT LEG (make two):
Using 4mm (UK 8; US 6) needles, cast on 6 sts in yarn A.
Row 1 (RS): (kfb) six times (12 sts).
Row 2: purl.
Row 3: (k1, kfb) six times (18 sts).
Rows 4–18: St st. Place a stitch marker here.
Row 19: k2tog, k14, k2tog (16 sts).
Row 20: purl.
Row 21: k2tog, k12, k2tog (14 sts).
Row 22: purl.
Row 23: k2tog, k10, k2tog (12 sts).
Row 24: purl.
Row 25: k2tog, k8, k2tog (10 sts).
Row 26: purl.
Row 27: (k2tog) five times (5 sts).
Cast/bind off purlwise.

PAW (make two):
Using 4mm (UK 8; US 6) needles, cast on 16 sts in yarn A.
Rows 1 (WS)–5: St st starting with a p row.
Row 6: (k2, k2tog) four times (12 sts).
Row 7: purl.
Row 8: (k2tog) six times (6 sts).
Break yarn and thread through rem sts, pull tight and fasten off securely.

REAR RIGHT LEG:
Using 4mm (UK 8; US 6) needles, cast on 6 sts in yarn A.
Row 1 (WS): purl.
Row 2: (kfb) six times (12 sts).
Row 3: purl.
Row 4: (k1, kfb) six times (18 sts).
Row 5: purl.
Row 6: (k2, kfb) six times (24 sts).
Rows 7–15: St st starting with a p row.
Row 16: k9 sts then transfer these to a stitch holder, k13, k2tog (14 sts).
Row 17: purl.
Row 18: k2tog, k10, k2tog (12 sts).
Row 19: purl.

Row 20: k2tog, k8, k2tog (10 sts).
Row 21: (p2tog) five times (5 sts).
Break yarn and thread through rem sts, pull tight and fasten off securely.
Return to sts on stitch holder, with WS facing:
Row 1 (WS): cast on 9 sts, p9 from stitch holder (18 sts).
Rows 2–7: St st starting with a k row.
Row 8: (k2, kfb) six times (24 sts).
Rows 9–11: St st starting with a p row.
Row 12: (k2, k2tog) six times (18 sts).
Row 13: purl.
Row 14: (k1, k2tog) six times (12 sts).
Row 15: (p2tog) six times (6 sts).
Break yarn and thread through rem sts, pull tight and secure.

REAR LEFT LEG:
Using 4mm (UK 8; US 6) needles, cast on 6 sts in yarn A.
Row 1 (WS): purl.
Row 2: (kfb) six times (12 sts).
Row 3: purl.
Row 4: (k1, kfb) six times (18 sts).
Row 5: purl.
Row 6: (k2, kfb) six times (24 sts).
Rows 7–15: St st starting with a p row.
Row 16: k2tog, k13, *turn*, leaving rem 9 sts unworked (14 sts).
Row 17: purl.
Row 18: k2tog, k10, k2tog (12 sts).
Row 19: purl.
Row 20: k2tog, k8, k2tog (10 sts).
Row 21: (p2tog) five times (5 sts).
Break yarn and thread through rem sts, pull tight and fasten off securely.

Note: *this next section is working from the hip to the foot, using the unworked stitches from Row 16.*
Return to rem unworked sts, with RS facing:
Row 1 (RS): cast on 9 sts, k9 rem sts (18 sts).
Rows 2–6: St st.
Row 7: (k2, kfb) six times (24 sts).
Rows 8–10: St st.
Row 11: (k2, k2tog) six times (18 sts).
Row 12: purl.
Row 13: (k1, k2tog) six times (12 sts).
Row 14: (p2tog) six times (6 sts).
Break yarn and thread through rem sts, pull tight and fasten off securely.

STAGE 2: SEWING UP

1. With right sides facing, sew together the row ends of the body with yarn A, leaving a 5–6cm (2–2½in) gap in the middle for stuffing into later.

2. With right sides facing, sew together the row ends of the head with yarn A, leaving the cast-on edge open to create a small cup shape.

3. With right sides facing, sew together the row ends of the muzzle with yarn A, leaving the cast-on edge open to create a pointed cone shape.

4. With right sides facing, sew together the row ends of the front legs between Rows 19 (marker) and 27 (the bottom of the foot), using yarn A.

5. With right sides facing, fold over the smaller 'foot' sections of each sitting rear leg to form open cup shapes. Following the diagram below for the shape and indication of where to sew, use yarn A to sew together the row ends of each foot.

6. Sew together the row ends of the front paws with yarn A, leaving the cast-on edges open to create two small cup shapes.

7. With right sides facing, sew together the row ends of the tail, leaving the cast-on edge open to create a test-tube shape.

8. Fasten in all loose ends as these can get in the way when felting. Turn all the hollow shapes the right way out.

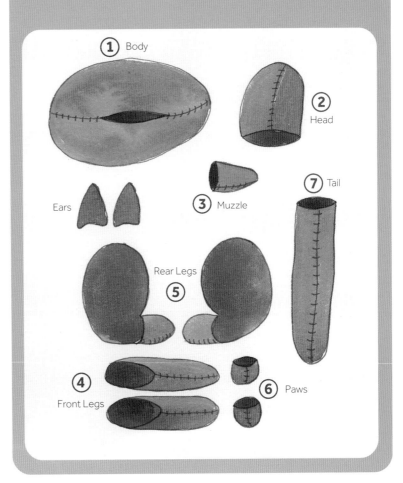

STAGE 3: WET FELTING

1. Wet felt the body and head, following the information on page 30.

2. Wet felt the remaining body pieces, following the information on page 31.

3. When all the pieces are felted equally, rinse them off. Pull the ears into shape; the remaining hollow pieces (and the feet of the rear legs) can be stuffed with kitchen roll.

4. Leave all the pieces to dry completely.

STAGE 4: STUFFING & CONSTRUCTION

1. Stuff the body firmly and sew up the gap with yarn A.

2. Stuff the head. Pin it to the body as indicated on the diagram. Sew the head in place with yarn A using small, close stitches. Add extra stuffing before sewing up completely, if required.

3. Stuff the muzzle and pin it to the head, referring to the diagram. When you are happy with your positioning, sew the muzzle in place with yarn A using small, close stitches. Add extra stuffing before sewing up completely, if required.

4. Stuff the paws then position and pin each one onto the closed, rounded ends of the front legs, using the diagram to help you. When you are happy with your positioning, sew the paws in place with yarn A using small, close stitches. Add extra stuffing before sewing up completely, if required.

5. Stuff the front legs and the feet of the rear legs, then position and pin them onto the body as shown in the diagram. Take some time with the pinning process, to ensure that Ember sits steadily on a flat surface. When you are happy with your positioning, sew the front and rear legs in place with yarn A. Add extra stuffing before sewing the legs up completely, especially in the 'hips' of the rear legs.

6. Make a small stitch across the points of each ear to pinch them in and make them pointier. Position and pin the ears onto the upper sides of the head as shown in the diagram. Sew the bases in place with yarn A.

7. Position, pin and sew the tail to the bottom of Ember's body with yarn A, as shown on the diagram. Ember should be slightly sitting on his own tail! For this reason, make sure that the body is still stable and the feet touch the ground.

STAGE 5: NEEDLE FELTING & DETAILS

1. The red-brown coloured yarn makes a lovely base colour for the fox but needs toning down, so I suggest attaching a thin, base layer of fur in a lighter colour to not only subdue the colour but add further, subtle blends of colour. Following the base flat fur instructions on page 39, needle felt a thin layer of mustard-mix merino wool tops all over the head, muzzle, tops of the front and rear legs, ears and tail.

2. Add charcoal wool roving to the lower portions of the front legs and on the feet of the back legs, following the base flat fur instructions on page 39. As you reach the intersection between the lower and upper legs, try to create a feathered effect with the charcoal wool roving to suggest a smooth, feathered graduation towards the mustard-mix merino wool tops – pulling off wispier fibres and varying how high they sit along the intersection helps to achieve this.

3. At the end of the muzzle, and on the chest and tummy, needle felt flat a layer of natural white fleece, following the base flat fur instructions on page 39.

4. Add natural white fleece to the neck, chest and end of the tail, following the 'bouncy' fur instructions on page 40. Around the neck, work mostly around the centre and leave the ends loose, to give Ember's neck fur a fluffier texture.

5. Needle felt thin amounts of natural white fleece inside the ears, referring to the instructions on page 54. Over each white inner ear, lay and needle felt a tiny, wispy length of charcoal wool roving, to add a line of shadowing at the centre. Remember – when working on the ears, use a foam block or rice bag to protect your fingers.

6. Add a ring of tufty, rusty fur around the top of the white, fleecy end of the tail with the mustard-mix merino wool tops, following the instructions on page 42.

7. Create the eye sockets for Ember, following the instructions on page 48.

8. To build up and fill in the centre of the face from the forehead to the end of the muzzle sculpt a nose, referring to the instructions on page 50. At the top of the bridge of the nose, fan out the fibres ever so slightly.

9. Make detailed eyes for Ember, using the instructions on page 51 as a guide: the order of merino wool tops colours, from base to top, is brown, black then white.

10. Add eyebrows with the mustard mix merino wool tops, following the instructions in steps 1 and 2 on page 52.

11. Referring to the Linear Details instructions on page 54, twist two lengths of black merino wool tops and 'draw' these over the top of each eye, to create eyelash lines and complete the eyes.

12. Add a shaped nose with the black merino wool tops, following the instructions on page 53.

13. 'Draw' the lines of the mouth with twisted black merino wool tops, following the Linear Details instructions on page 54.

14. Finish Ember's face by attaching layered, folded white and mustard-mix merino wool tops to each side of the face to create 'whiskers', following the Colour Blending instructions on pages 46 and 47.

15. Using some black or charcoal yarn, sew the toes onto each front paw, following the information on page 56.

16. Sew the feet of the front paws together with a few tiny anchor stitches using yarn A. Secure the tail to the side of the rear leg with a few anchor stitches, again using yarn A.

ROSEMARY & THYME
THE SQUIRRELS

These red (Rosemary) and grey (Thyme) squirrels are great friends and love to collect acorns together! Use the same pattern for either squirrel; the only differences are the ears and the yarn and fibre colours. Neither squirrel requires a base layer of fur made with fibre, as I felt the texture of the felted knitting alone suited the natural fur on a real squirrel.

Difficulty

- Intermediate

What you need

- Yarn
  ▷ 65g (2¼oz) of Woolyknit Aran in Rust **OR** Light Grey Natural, or equivalent aran (worsted) weight 100% pure wool yarn in red-brown **OR** variegated light-grey; 50g/85yd/77m **[A]**
- Felting fibres
  ▷ Red-brown (**only for Rosemary**), dark-brown, light-brown, black and white merino wool tops
  ▷ Natural white fleece
  ▷ Natural-grey and mauve wool roving (**only for Thyme**)
- Toy filling
- Stitch holder
- Stitch marker (a contrasting-coloured scrap of yarn makes a handy, economical alternative)

Needles

- One pair of 5mm (UK 6; US 8) needles
- Tapestry needle
- Set of three needle-felting needles in sizes 40, 38 and 32

Tension/gauge

- 18 sts x 24 rows in a 10cm (4in) square over St st, using 5mm (UK 6; US 8) needles

INSTRUCTIONS

STAGE 1: THE KNIT BIT

BODY:
Using 5mm (UK 6; US 8) needles, cast on 8 sts in yarn A.
Row 1 (RS): (kfb) eight times (16 sts).
Row 2: purl.
Row 3: (k1, kfb) eight times (24 sts).
Row 4: purl.
Row 5: (k2, kfb) eight times (32 sts).
Row 6: purl.
Row 7: (k3, kfb) eight times (40 sts).
Rows 8-14: St st.
Row 15: (k4, kfb) eight times (48 sts).
Rows 16-20: St st.
Row 21: (k4, k2tog) eight times (40 sts).
Row 22: purl.
Row 23: (k3, k2tog) eight times (32 sts).
Row 24: purl.
Row 25: (k2, k2tog) eight times (24 sts).
Row 26: purl.
Row 27: (k1, k2tog) eight times (16 sts).
Row 28: purl.
Row 29: (k2tog) eight times (8 sts).
Break yarn and thread through rem sts, pull tight and fasten off securely.

EAR (make two):
Rosemary (red squirrel)
Using 5mm (UK 6; US 8) needles, cast on 8 sts in yarn A.
Row 1 (RS): knit
Row 2: purl.
Cast/bind off.

Thyme (grey squirrel)
Using 5mm (UK 6; US 8) needles, cast on 6 sts in yarn A.
Row 1: purl.
Row 2: k5, kfb (7 sts).
Row 3: purl.
Row 4: k5, k2tog (6 sts).
Cast/bind off.

HEAD:
Using 5mm (UK 6; US 8) needles, cast on 4 sts in yarn A.
Row 1 (RS): (kfb) five times (8 sts).
Row 2: purl.
Row 3: (k1, kfb) four times (12 sts).
Row 4: purl.
Row 5: (k2, kfb) four times (16 sts).
Row 6: purl.
Row 7: (k3, kfb) four times (20 sts).
Row 8: purl.
Row 9: (k4, kfb) four times (24 sts).
Rows 10-12: St st.
Row 13: (k4, k2tog) four times (20 sts).
Row 14: purl.
Row 15: (k3, k2tog) four times (16 sts).
Rows 16-18: St st.
Row 19: (k2, k2tog) four times (12 sts).
Rows 20-22: St st.
Row 23: (k1, k2tog) four times (8 sts).
Row 24: purl.
Row 25: (k2tog) four times (4 sts).
Break yarn and thread through rem sts, pull tight and fasten off securely.

ARM (make two):
Using 5mm (UK 6; US 8) needles, cast on 6 sts in yarn A.
Row 1 (WS): purl.
Row 2: kfb, k4, kfb (8 sts).
Rows 3-5: St st starting with a p row.
Row 6: place stitch marker, kfb, k6, kfb (10 sts).
Rows 7-11: St st starting with a p row.
Row 12: k2tog, k6, k2tog (8 sts).
Row 13-15: St st starting with a p row.
Row 16: (k2, k2tog) twice (6 sts).
Break yarn and thread through rem sts, pull tight and fasten off securely.

LEFT LEG:
Using 5mm (UK 6; US 8) needles, cast on 4 sts in yarn A.
Row 1 (RS): (kfb) four times (8 sts).
Row 2: purl.
Row 3: (k1, kfb) four times (12 sts).
Row 4: purl.
Row 5: (k2, kfb) four times (16 sts).
Rows 6-10: St st.
Row 11: k2tog, k8, turn, leaving rem 6 sts unworked (9 sts).
Row 12: purl.
Row 13: k2tog, k5, k2tog (7 sts).
Row 14: purl.
Row 15: k2tog, k3, k2tog (5 sts).
Break yarn and thread through rem sts, pull tight and fasten off securely.

Note: *this next section is working from the hip towards the toe, using the unworked stitches on Row 11.*
Row 1: with RS facing, cast on 6 sts at beg of row, k rem sts from Row 11 (12 sts).
Rows 2-8: St st.
Row 9: (k2tog) six times (6 sts).
Row 10: purl.
Break yarn and thread through rem sts, pull tight and fasten off securely.

RIGHT LEG:
Using 5mm (UK 6; US 8) needles, cast on 4 sts in yarn A.
Row 1 (RS): (kfb) four times (8 sts).
Row 2: purl.
Row 3: (k1, kfb) four times (12 sts).
Row 4: purl.
Row 5: (k2, kfb) four times (16 sts).
Rows 6-10: St st starting with a p row.
Row 11: k6 and place these sts on a stitch holder, k8, k2tog (9 sts).
Row 12: purl.
Row 13: k2tog, k5, k2tog (7 sts).
Row 14: purl.
Row 15: k2tog, k3, k2tog (5 sts).
Row 16 (WS): cast on 6 sts at beg of row, p rem sts from Row 11 (12 sts).
Rows 17-24: St st.
Row 25: (k2tog) six times (6 sts).
Break yarn and thread through rem sts, pull tight and fasten off securely.

TAIL:
Using 5mm (UK 6; US 8) needles, cast on 8 sts in yarn A.
Row 1 (WS): purl.
Row 2: (k1, kfb) four times (12 sts).
Row 3: purl.
Row 4: (k1, kfb) six times (18 sts).

Rows 5–7: St st starting with a p row.
Row 8: (k2, kfb) six times (24 sts).
Rows 9–19: St st starting with a p row.
Row 20: k2tog, k20, k2tog (22 sts).
Rows 21–23: St st starting with a p row.
Row 24: k2tog, k18, k2tog (20 sts).
Rows 25–27: St st starting with a p row.
Row 28: k2tog, k16, k2tog (18 sts).
Rows 29–37: St st starting with a p row.
Row 38: k2tog, k14, k2tog (16 sts).
Row 39: purl.
Row 40: k2tog, k12, k2tog (14 sts).
Rows 41–45: St st starting with a p row.
Row 46: kfb, k12, kfb (16 sts).
Row 47: purl.
Row 48: kfb, k14, kfb (18 sts).
Rows 49–55: St st starting with a p row.
Row 56: (k2tog) nine times (9 sts).
Break yarn and thread through rem sts, pull tight and fasten off securely.

STAGE 2: SEWING UP

1. With right sides facing, sew together the row ends of the body with yarn A, leaving a 5–6cm (2–2½in) gap in the middle for stuffing into later.

2. With right sides facing, sew together the row ends of the head with yarn A, leaving a 4cm (1½in) gap in the middle for stuffing into later.

3. With right sides facing, sew together the row ends of the arms between Rows 6 (marker) and 16 (the paw end) with yarn A.

4. With right sides facing, fold over the smaller 'foot' sections of each sitting rear leg to form open cup shapes. Following the diagram below for the shape and indication of where to sew, use yarn A to sew together the row ends of each foot.

5. With right sides facing, sew together the row ends of the tail with yarn A, leaving the cast-on edge open.

6. Fasten in all loose ends as these can get in the way when felting. Turn all the hollow shapes the right way out.

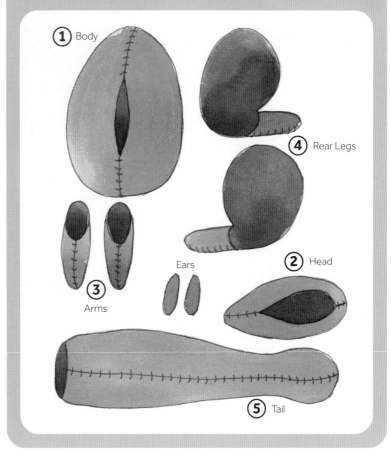

(1) Body
(4) Rear Legs
(2) Head
(3) Arms
Ears
(5) Tail

STAGE 3: WET FELTING

1. Wet felt the body, tail and head, following the information on page 30.

2. Wet felt the remaining body pieces, following the information on page 31.

3. Wet a small amount of light-brown merino wool tops for the acorn, following the technique below.

4. When all pieces are felted equally, rinse them off. Pull the ears into shape; the remaining hollow pieces (and the feet of the rear legs) can be stuffed with kitchen roll.

5. Leave all pieces to dry completely.

Acorns

These are made with small lengths of your chosen coloured fibre, gently pulled off wool roving or merino wool tops and then rolled up into a ball. As only a little water is needed, you can use just a small bowl for your hot water and washing-up liquid.

1. Pull off an 8cm (3in) length of 1cm (⅜in) wide small strip of fibres. Tie them with the knot at the centre – this secures the fibres together, and forms a densely wrapped shape.

2. Roll the knotted fibres into a ball. Sprinkle a little of the hot soapy water over the top – too much, and your ball will become too soapy and sloppy!

3. Begin to roll the ball between the palms of your hands, gently at first and gradually building up the pressure to make a round, firm sphere. This forms the nut of the acorn; its cap will be added later, at the needle-felting stage.

STAGE 4: STUFFING & CONSTRUCTION

1. Stuff the body firmly and sew up the gap with yarn A.

2. Stuff the head and pin it into position on top of the body, as indicated on the diagram. Sew it in place with yarn A using small, close stitches. Add extra stuffing before completely closing up, if required.

3. Stuff the arms lightly to keep them slim. Position, pin and sew them in place to each side of the body with yarn A.

4. Stuff the feet of the rear legs then pin them into position on the body, as shown in the diagram.

5. When stuffing the tail, make it full and firm but leave the bottom 4cm (1½in) empty, as this section will be attached flat to the lower back area of your squirrel, as indicated in the diagram. Pin the tail into position, so the base is flat against the squirrel's base and curls up around the back of the squirrel.

6. Take the time to reposition the rear legs and tail at this point, if needed, to ensure your squirrel sits steadily on a flat surface. Once you are happy with their positioning, sew them in place with yarn A. As you sew on the rear legs, add extra stuffing to the 'hips' before sewing them up completely. For the tail, sew the sides and bottom to the back of the squirrel with yarn A using small, close stitches. Leave the top curved section loose. At the 'neck' of the tail, between the rounded, loose top and sewn-on section, make a few stitches with yarn A then pull the yarn to draw the two sections together, to form a curved tail.

7. Position, pin and sew on the ears with yarn A: Rosemary (the red squirrel) has smaller, slimmer ears which face forward; Thyme (the grey squirrel) has larger, rounder ears and the inner ears face towards the sides.

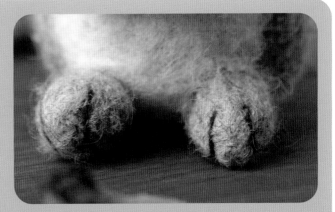

STAGE 5: NEEDLE FELTING & DETAILS

1. Following the instructions on page 39 for base flat fur, needle felt natural white fleece under the base of the head, down the neck, around the chest and right down to the tummy of either squirrel until you reach the base of the tail. This not only gives your squirrel a white chest and tummy, but it also covers up the stitches from Stage 4.

2. Using either red-brown merino wool tops for Rosemary or natural-grey wool roving for Thyme, needle felt the fibres to the lower, sewn-on portion of the tail, following the instructions for base flat fur on page 39. To make this lower section fluffier, flick your needle over the fibres, referring to the Fluffy Fur instructions on page 40.

3. For the top portion where the tail is bent over, follow the instructions for the Short, Tufty Fur technique on page 42, using either the red-brown merino wool tops (Rosemary) or natural-grey wool roving (Thyme). Work from bottom to top, to create an effective, layered, tufty texture.

4. Make detailed eyes for Rosemary or Thyme, using the instructions on page 51 as a guide. The order of merino wool tops colours for Rosemary, from bottom to top, is black then white; for Thyme, it is dark-brown then white.

5. For Rosemary, I have added an outline around the eyes to give them further definition. Following the step 1 information in the Linear Details instructions on page 54, make a thin strand with the light-brown merino wool tops and needle felt this all around the eye.

For Thyme, repeat the process for the outline above but using the white merino wool tops instead. In addition, use the same linear detail technique to add an eyelash line along the top of the eye, using the black merino wool tops.

6. Follow the instructions for the Linear Details once again to create the mouth and paw details, using the dark-brown merino wool tops.

7. To finish off the acorn, needle felt either the dark-brown merino wool tops (for Rosemary) or the mauve wool roving (for Thyme) around the lower portion of the wet felted acorn ball made earlier, to make the cup. Stitch the acorn between the front paws with yarn A. Add a little extra dark-brown merino wool tops or mauve wool roving to hide any stitches that may be visible.

BISCUIT THE SCHNAUZER

Biscuit is a beautiful little fella: with his well-groomed ears and tufty tummy, he is adorable and stylish! He is knitted with aran (worsted) weight yarn, which means you will have good-sized chunky pieces to work with. The needle felting looks a lot more complicated than it is, so he will make a great project for impressing your friends!

Difficulty

• Easy to Intermediate

What you need

• Yarn

▷ *90g (3¼oz) of Drops Alaska in Grey Mix, or equivalent aran (worsted) weight 100% pure wool yarn in grey; 50g/77yd/70m [A]*

• Felting fibres

▷ *Brown, steel-grey, black and white merino wool tops*
▷ *Grey wool roving*
▷ *Natural white fleece*

• Toy filling

Needles

• One pair of 5mm (UK 6; US 8) needles
• Tapestry needle
• Set of three needle-felting needles in sizes 40, 38 and 32

Tension/gauge

• 17 sts x 22 rows in a 10cm (4in) square over St st, using 5mm (UK 6; US 8) needles

INSTRUCTIONS

STAGE 1: THE KNIT BIT

BODY:
Using 5mm (UK 6; US 8) needles, cast on 6 sts in yarn A.
Row 1 (WS): purl.
Row 2: (kfb) six times (12 sts).
Row 3: purl.
Row 4: (k1, kfb) six times (18 sts).
Row 5: purl.
Row 6: (k2, kfb) six times (24 sts).
Row 7: purl.
Row 8: (k3, kfb) six times (30 sts).
Row 9: purl.
Row 10: (k4, kfb) six times (36 sts).
Row 11: purl.
Row 12: (k5, kfb) six times (42 sts).
Row 13: purl.
Row 14: (k6, kfb) six times (48 sts).
Rows 15–19: St st starting with a p row.
Row 20: (k6, k2tog) six times (42 sts).
Rows 21–23: st st starting with a p row.
Row 24: (k5, k2tog) six times (36 sts).
Rows 25–33: st st starting with a p row.
Row 34: (k5, kfb) six times (42 sts).
Rows 35–41: St st starting with a p row.
Row 42: (k5, k2tog) six times (36 sts).
Row 43: purl.
Row 44: (k4, k2tog) six times (30 sts).
Row 45: purl.
Row 46: (k3, k2tog) six times (24 sts).
Row 47: purl.
Row 48: (k2, k2tog) six times (18 sts).
Row 49: purl.
Row 50: (k1, k2tog) six times (12 sts).
Row 51: purl.
Row 52: (k2tog) six times (6 sts).
Break yarn and thread through rem sts, pull tight and fasten off securely.

HEAD:
Using 5mm (UK 6; US 8) needles, cast on 30 sts in yarn A.
Rows 1 (WS)–17: St st starting with a p row.
Row 18: (k3, k2tog) six times (24 sts).
Row 19–21: St st starting with a p row.

Row 22: (k2, k2tog) six times (18 sts).
Row 23: purl.
Row 24: (k1, k2tog) six times (12 sts).
Break yarn and thread through rem sts, pull tight and fasten off securely.

EAR (make two):
Using 5mm (UK 6; US 8) needles, cast on 6 sts in yarn A.
Row 1 (WS): purl.
Row 2: kfb, k4, kfb (8 sts).
Row 3: purl.
Row 4: kfb, k6, kfb (10 sts).
Rows 5–7: St st starting with a p row.
Row 8: k2tog, k6, k2tog (8 sts).
Rows 9–11: St st starting with a p row.
Row 12: k2tog, k4, k2tog (6 sts).
Row 13: purl.
Row 14: k2tog, k2, k2tog (4 sts).
Row 15: purl.
Row 16: (k2tog) twice (2 sts).
Break yarn and thread through rem sts, pull tight and fasten off securely.

MUZZLE:
Using 5mm (UK 6; US 8) needles, cast on 16 sts in yarn A.
Rows 1 (WS)–7: St st starting with a p row.
Row 8: k1, (k1, k2tog) five times (11 sts).
Row 9: purl.
Row 10: k1, (k2tog) five times (6 sts).
Break yarn and thread through rem sts, pull tight and fasten off securely.

FRONT LEG (make two):
Using 5mm (UK 6; US 8) needles, cast on 14 sts in yarn A.
Rows 1 (WS)–5: St st starting with a p row.
Row 6: k2tog, k10, k2tog (12 sts).
Rows 7–11: St st starting with a p row.
Row 12: k9, turn.
Row 13: p6, turn.
Row 14: k5, k2tog, turn.
Row 15: p5, p2tog, turn.
Rows 16–19: rep last 2 rows twice more (6 sts).

Rows 20 and 21: St st.
Row 22: k2tog, k2, k2tog (4 sts).
Row 23: purl.
Row 24: (k2tog) twice (2 sts).
Row 25: purl.
Break yarn and thread through rem sts, pull tight and fasten off securely.

REAR LEG (make two):
Using 5mm (UK 6; US 8) needles, cast on 16 sts in yarn A.
Rows 1 (WS)–5: St st starting with a p row.
Row 6: k2tog, k12, k2tog (14 sts).
Rows 7–15: St st starting with a p row.
Row 16: k11, turn.
Row 17: p8, turn.
Row 18: k7, k2tog, turn.
Row 19: p7, p2tog, turn.
Rows 20–23: rep last 2 rows twice more (8 sts).
Rows 24–25: St st.
Row 26: k2tog, k4, k2tog (6 sts).
Row 27: p2tog, p2, p2tog (4 sts).
Row 28: (k2tog) twice (2 sts).
Row 29: purl.
Break yarn and thread through rem sts, pull tight and fasten off securely.

TAIL:
Using 5mm (UK 6; US 8) needles, cast on 10 sts in yarn A.
Rows 1 (WS)–17: St st starting with a p row.
Row 18: k2tog, k6, k2tog (8 sts).
Row 19–21: St st starting with a p row.
Row 22: k2tog, k4, k2tog (6 sts).
Row 23–25: St st starting with a p row.
Row 26: k2tog, k2, k2tog (4 sts).
Row 27: purl.
Break yarn and thread through rem sts, pull tight and fasten off securely.

STAGE 2: SEWING UP

1. With right sides facing, sew together the row ends of the body with yarn A, leaving a 5–6cm (2–2½in) gap in the middle for stuffing into later.

2. With right sides facing, sew together the row ends of the head with yarn A, leaving the cast-on edge open to form a cup shape.

3. With right sides facing, sew together the row ends of the muzzle with yarn A, leaving the cast-on edge open to form a cup shape.

4. With the right sides facing, sew up the front and rear legs, using the diagram, right, and the instructions on page 26 to help you: fold the leg in half from the point of the toe, then turn in the toe. Sew up the length of the leg and each side of the foot.

5. With right sides facing, sew together the row ends of the tail, working from the cast-on edge towards the point. Leave the cast-on edge open for stuffing later.

6. Fasten in all loose ends as these can get in the way when felting. Turn all the hollow shapes the right way out.

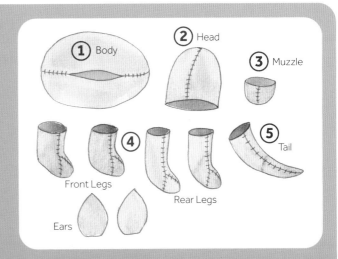

① Body ② Head ③ Muzzle ④ Front Legs Rear Legs ⑤ Tail Ears

STAGE 3: WET FELTING

1. Wet felt the body and head, following the information on page 30.

2. Wet felt the remaining pieces, following the information on page 31.

3. When all the pieces are felted equally, rinse them off. Pull the ears into shape; the remaining hollow pieces can be stuffed with kitchen roll.

4. Leave all the pieces to dry completely.

STAGE 4: STUFFING & CONSTRUCTION

1. Stuff the body firmly and sew up the space left in the tummy with yarn A.

2. Stuff the head and pin it into position, referring to the diagram. When you are happy with your positioning, sew the head to the body with yarn A using small, close stitches. Add extra stuffing before completely sewing on the head, if required.

3. Lightly stuff the muzzle then pin it into position on the head, using the diagram to help you – note, the seam edge should be facing down. When you are happy with your positioning, sew the muzzle to the head with yarn A using small, close stitches. Add extra stuffing before completely sewing on the muzzle, if required.

4. Stuff the front and rear legs then pin them into position onto the base of the body, as shown in the diagram – note, the rear legs are slightly longer and should sit a little higher at the back of the body. Take some time to reposition the legs, if necessary, to ensure Biscuit sits steadily on a flat surface. When you are happy with your positioning, sew the legs in place with yarn A using small, close stitches. Add extra stuffing before completely sewing on each leg, if required.

5. Stuff the tail (use the tip of a knitting needle to help squish the stuffing right down to the pointed end) then pin it at the back of body. Sew it in place with yarn A using small, close stitches.

6. Position and pin the ears so that the points of the ears face backwards, as shown in the diagram. Sew the base in place with yarn A [**6a**]. Once the ears are secure, fold each ear point over, so that they face downwards, as shown in the diagram [**6b**]. Secure the folded ears with small stitches in yarn A, taken from the outer ear then into and out of the head.

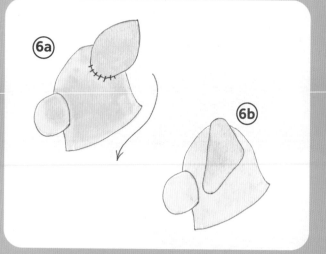

STAGE 5: NEEDLE FELTING & DETAILS

1. I liked the knitted texture of my schnauzer, so decided to needle felt only a few fibres onto his body, here and there, to hide any obvious seams. Using the instructions for base flat fur on page 39 as a guide, pull short, thin lengths of grey wool roving and needle felt them in any places where you want to hide any stitches from Stage 4. Stab them in thoroughly until the fibres are fully integrated.

2. Add natural white fleece to Biscuit's tummy, chest and bottom areas, following the instructions for short tufty, fur on page 42.

3. Using a combination of grey wool roving and natural white fleece, add the fluffy hair along Biscuit's chest and around each paw, following the Colour Blending instructions on pages 46 and 47.

4. Using a combination of grey wool roving and black merino wool tops, add the fluffy hair along each side of Biscuit's body, following the Colour Blending instructions on pages 46 and 47.

5. Add flat layers of natural white fleece to the underside of the tail and the backs of the legs, following the base flat fur instructions on page 39.

6. To add the beard, follow the Colour Blending instructions on pages 46 and 47. Begin by adding the beard at the sides of the muzzle, working from the chin to the top of the muzzle and using a combination of grey wool roving, a little of the black and steel-grey merino wool tops and natural white fleece. Repeat the process for the front of the muzzle, below the nose area, using a mix of grey wool roving, tiny wisps of brown merino wool tops and natural white fleece.

7. Finish the muzzle by needle felting a strip of grey wool roving horizontally over the top of the muzzle, as per steps 8–10 on page 47.

8. Make the eye sockets for Biscuit, referring to the instructions on page 48.

9. Make detailed eyes for Biscuit, using the instructions on page 51 as a guide: the order of merino wool tops colours, from base to top, is black, brown, black then white.

10. Using a combination of little amounts of grey wool roving, steel-grey and black merino wool tops and natural white fleece, create an eyebrow for Biscuit by following the Colour Blending instructions on pages 46 and 47. Attach the fibres in a single line, then trim them so that the eyebrow is longer at the front, near the eyes, and gradually gets shorter towards the back, between the ears.

11. For the nose, create a large, firm, oval shape with the black merino wool tops by folding under the top and bottom edges of the strip of fibres and rolling it gently between your palms. Using the main picture on page 149 as a guide for placement, needle felt the nose into position: work around the outer edges first then lightly needle felt the middle here and there – you want to keep the shape as rounded and full at the centre as possible.

PAPRIKA THE HIGHLAND COW

Paprika is so on trend, with her curly locks and jaunty horns! She is surprisingly easy to make – with just a few simple knitted pieces and nifty techniques, you can create a stunning and unique little creature to roam your home.

Difficulty

- Easy

What you need

- Yarn

▷ 85g (3oz) of Drops Alaska in Light Brown Mix, or equivalent aran (worsted) weight 100% pure wool yarn in variegated light-brown; 50g/77yd/70m *[A]*
▷ Small amount of black yarn, for sewing the hooves

- Felting fibres

▷ Red-brown, dark-brown, steel-grey, black and white merino wool tops
▷ Mauve and tan-brown wool roving
▷ Natural white fleece

- Toy filling
- 12cm (4¾in) length of 1.5mm (0.06in/15 gauge) wire

Needles

- One pair of 5mm (UK 6; US 8) needles
- Tapestry needle
- Set of three needle-felting needles in sizes 40, 38 and 32

Tension/gauge

- 17 sts x 22 rows in a 10cm (4in) square over St st, using 5mm (UK 6; US 8) needles

INSTRUCTIONS

STAGE 1: THE KNIT BIT

BODY:
Using 5mm (UK 6; US 8) needles, cast on 6 sts in yarn A.
Row 1 (WS): (kfb) six times (12 sts).
Row 2: purl.
Row 3: (kfb) twelve times (24 sts).
Row 4: purl.
Row 5: (k1, kfb) twelve times (36 sts).
Rows 6-8: St st.
Row 9: (k5, kfb) six times (42 sts).
Row 10: purl.
Row 11: (k6, kfb) six times (48 sts).
Rows 12-18: St st.
Row 19: (k6, k2tog) six times (42 sts).
Rows 20-28: St st.
Row 29: (k5, k2tog) six times (36 sts).
Row 30-34: St st.
Row 35: (k5, kfb) six times (42 sts).
Rows 36-44: St st.
Row 45: (k5, k2tog) six times (36 sts).
Row 46: purl.
Row 47: (k1, k2tog) twelve times (24 sts).
Row 48: purl.
Row 49: (k2tog) twelve times (12 sts).
Row 50: purl.
Row 51: (k2tog) six times (6 sts).
Break yarn and thread through rem sts, pull tight and fasten off securely.

HEAD:
Using 5mm (UK 6; US 8) needles, cast on 24 sts in yarn A.
Row 1 (W): purl.
Row 2: (k2, kfb) eight times (32 sts).
Rows 3-7: St st starting with a p row.
Row 8: (k2, k2tog) eight times (24 sts).
Row 9: purl.
Row 10: (k2tog) twelve times (12 sts).
Row 11: purl.
Row 12: (k2tog) six times (6 sts).
Break yarn and thread through rem sts, pull tight and fasten off securely.

MUZZLE:
Using 5mm (UK 6; US 8) needles, cast on 16 sts in yarn A.
Row 1 (RS): kfb, k14, kfb (18 sts).
Rows 2-4: St st.
Row 5: (k1, k2tog) six times (12 sts).
Row 6: purl.
Row 7: (k2tog) six times (6 sts).
Break yarn and thread through rem sts, pull tight and fasten off securely.

EAR (make two):
Using 5mm (UK 6; US 8) needles, cast on 7 sts in yarn A.
Rows 1 (WS)-3: St st starting with a p row.
Row 4: k2tog, k3, k2tog (5 sts).
Row 5: purl.
Row 6: k2tog, k1, k2tog (3 sts).
Break yarn and thread through rem sts, pull tight and fasten off securely.

FRONT LEG (make two):
Using 5mm (UK 6; US 8) needles, cast on 12 sts in yarn A.
Rows 1 (WS)-3: St st starting with a p row.
Row 4: k2tog, k8, k2tog (10 sts).
Rows 5-13: St st starting with a p row.
Row 14: k2tog, k6, k2tog (8 sts).
Row 15: purl.
Break yarn and thread through rem sts, pull tight and fasten off securely.

REAR LEG (make two)
Using 5mm (UK 6; US 8) needles, cast on 16 sts in yarn A.
Rows 1 (WS)-3: St st starting with a p row.
Row 4: k2tog, k12, k2tog (14 sts).
Rows 5-9: St st starting with a p row.
Row 10: k2tog, k10, k2tog (12 sts).
Row 11: purl.
Row 12: k2tog, k8, k2tog (10 sts).
Row 13: purl.
Row 14: k2tog, k6, k2tog (8 sts).
Row 15: purl.
Break yarn and thread through rem sts, pull tight and fasten off securely.

STAGE 2: SEWING UP

1. With right sides facing, sew together the row ends of the body with yarn A, leaving a 5–6cm (2–2½in) gap in the middle for stuffing into later.

2. With right sides facing, sew together the row ends of the head with yarn A, leaving the cast-on edge open to form a cup shape.

3. With right sides facing, sew together the row ends of the muzzle with yarn A, leaving the cast-on edge open to form a cup shape.

4. With the right sides facing, sew together the row ends of the front and rear legs with yarn A, leaving the cast-on edges open to form small cup shapes.

5. Fasten in all loose ends as these can get in the way when felting. Turn all the hollow shapes the right way out.

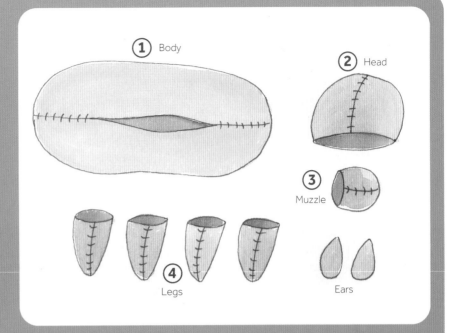

(1) Body
(2) Head
(3) Muzzle
(4) Legs
Ears

STAGE 3: WET FELTING

1. Wet felt the body and head, following the information on page 30.

2. Wet felt the rest of the pieces, following the information on page 31.

3. Create and wet felt the ringlets for Paprika with the brown merino wool tops, following the instructions on page 32.

4. Create and wet felt the horns for Paprika with the steel-grey merino wool tops, following the instructions on page 33.

5. When all the body pieces are wet felted equally, rinse them off. Pull the ears into shape; the remaining hollow pieces can be stuffed with kitchen roll.

6. Leave all the pieces to dry completely.

STAGE 4: STUFFING & CONSTRUCTION

1. Stuff the body firmly and sew up the space left in the tummy with yarn A.

2. Stuff the head and pin it into position, referring to the diagram. When you are happy with your positioning, sew the head to the body with yarn A using small, close stitches. Add extra stuffing before completely sewing on the head, if required.

3. Lightly stuff the muzzle then pin it into position on the head, using the diagram to help you – note, the seam edge should be facing down. When you are happy with your positioning, sew the muzzle to the head with yarn A using small, close stitches. Add extra stuffing before completely sewing on the muzzle, if required.

4. Stuff the front and rear legs then pin them into position onto the base of the body, as shown in the diagram – note, the rear legs are slightly wider and should sit a little higher at the back of the body. Take some time to reposition the legs, if necessary, to ensure Paprika stands steadily on a flat surface. When you are happy with your positioning,

sew the legs onto the body with yarn A, using small, close stitches. Add extra stuffing before completely sewing on each leg, if required.

5. Position, pin and sew the base of the ears in place with yarn A, using the diagram for reference.

STAGE 5: NEEDLE FELTING & DETAILS

1. Start by adding a layer of tan-brown wool roving to the head and legs, following the instructions for base flat fur on page 39.

2. Add a layer of tan-brown wool roving to the underside of the tummy, following the instructions for the 'bouncy' fur on page 40.

3. Cut a length of red-brown merino wool tops approximately 20–25cm (8–10in) long. Open out the fibres, so that they stretch along the full length of the top of Paprika's back and over her bottom. Attach by needle felting down the spine of the cow, in a line, from the neck to the tops of the rear legs. Secure the fibres at the sides of the body with random, light stabs – just so that they lie reasonably flat. Trim all round approximately 1cm (⅜in) longer than the body.

4. Follow the instructions on page 33 to attach the horns to Paprika's head.

5. The curls need to be added all over the body and on the top of the head. Following the instructions on page 41, attach the curly fur. Remember to attach each ringlet here and there only, to avoid over-felting them and making them lose their texture and shape.

6. Make eye sockets for Paprika, following the instructions on page 48.

7. Follow the instructions on page 51 to create detailed eyes for Paprika: the order of merino wool tops colours, from base to top, is dark-brown, black then white. Note that I have kept the base, dark-brown eye circular, and not stretched out the corners, as this makes Paprika's eyes look cuter!

8. Roll a small amount of mauve wool roving into an oval and needle felt this to the end of the muzzle, to create the nose. Roll two tiny balls of black merino wool tops and needle felt each one onto the nose, side-by-side, to create nostrils.

9. Work two to three overstitches through the end of each leg with the small amount of black yarn, to create hooves. Fasten off the yarn, following the instructions in step 7 on page 56.

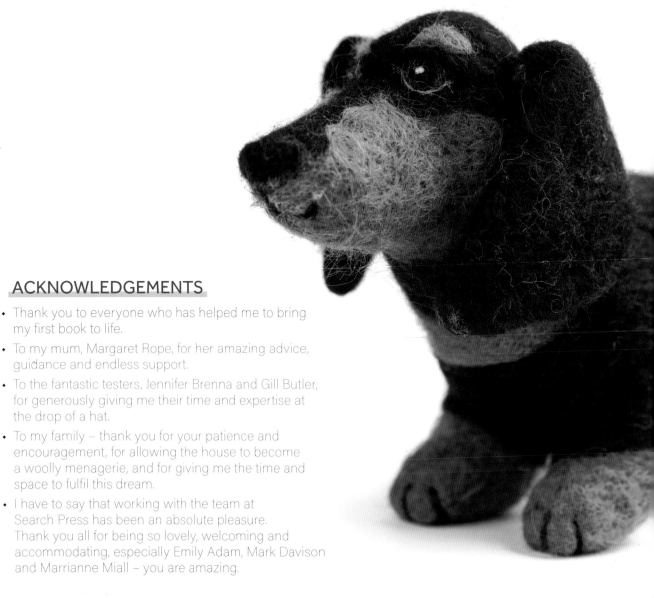

ACKNOWLEDGEMENTS

- Thank you to everyone who has helped me to bring my first book to life.
- To my mum, Margaret Rope, for her amazing advice, guidance and endless support.
- To the fantastic testers, Jennifer Brenna and Gill Butler, for generously giving me their time and expertise at the drop of a hat.
- To my family – thank you for your patience and encouragement, for allowing the house to become a woolly menagerie, and for giving me the time and space to fulfil this dream.
- I have to say that working with the team at Search Press has been an absolute pleasure. Thank you all for being so lovely, welcoming and accommodating, especially Emily Adam, Mark Davison and Marrianne Miall – you are amazing.